TRIAL
BY
FIRE

John Skinner

Gateways Publishing
Countess Wear, Exeter
ISBN -10 0-9553093-0-1
ISBN -13 972-0-9553093-0-4

Initial inputting:
Margaret Unsworth

Typesetting and Page Make-up:
David Banks

Scanning and Cover Design:
David Banks

Typeface: Garamond

Printed and bound in Great Britain by
Ashley House Printing Company, Exeter, Devon

Contents

To Marilyn, whose ministry of loving care, encouragement and support have made such a huge difference to all of us and not least throughout these testing days

*Re-prints of most of the photographs in this publication are available.
Email: david-banks@supanet.com for sizes and prices
*Re-prints are supplied as computer print-outs. Computer Print-outs left facing sunlight will fade. No guarantee is given or implied if fading occurs

Hywel and Sandra Jones at the Royal School for the Deaf. Our debt to them is immense and we thank God for them!

The photograph on the back cover shows the congregation of St. Leonard's Church meeting in the Royal School for the Deaf Assembly Hall. It was a tight squeeze , but wonderful times of fellowship. In some ways we were reluctant to move back into the refurbished church, the Lord had been good to us!

Illustrations

A

B

C

D

(I) Reconstruction work commences

(II) Charles Barker, who produced a scale model

(III) Arising from the ashes

(IV) The shape of things to come

(V) All systems go inside!

(VI) All systems go outside!

(VII) The Crazy Gang (there were times when it felt like that) hand over the restored Church

(VIII) A few of the key workers

E

(I) The splendid new entrance

(II) The team who produced the banner, still on view in the entrance hall

(III) The big day arrives and the Bishop comes to inspire us and dedicate the Centre

(IV) The Centre being used in a myriad of ways

(V) The Centre: a meeting ground

(VI) A few of the children who have an important role in the life of the church

(VII) And older folk, they should not be forgotten either

(VIII) Past, Present and with God's help a beacon of light for the Future

Foreward

My first visit to St. Leonard's, Exeter was in July 1958, though I do not recall now how I came by that invitation, but a year later, July 1959, saw me (a new driver) nervously trundling down from Bristol in a second-hand Ford Prefect, bearing Jim Packer to the wedding of John and Marilyn Skinner, where I was to give the address. John was Curate there and it was Marilyn's home church.

The wedding itself of course was wonderfully joyous, but sadly much Anglican worship had become stodgy in those far-off days, the services were repetitive, inflexible in style and quaint in language, and to the watching world belonged to another planet. How the Church of England has changed since those far-off days!

For many churches, liberation from this traditional bondage and clerical restrictive practices came slowly, but new publications such as Psalm Praise, published in 1973, brought a most welcome breath of fresh air. At that time it was accurately described as 'taking the psalms out of their corsets'. Things at last had begun to stir.

To help it on its way, St. Leonard's had the inestimable blessing of a divinely sent explosion. Like it or not, the past was irretrievably gone, and a blessed new era had dawned. Someone unknown had struck a match, but the Lord God Almighty had lit the fire!

I have simply loved reading John Skinner's account of that

event and the remarkable years that followed. I ended it moved to tears at the strange and wonderful ways of our God, the marvels of his grace, the open ear that never fails to hear our prayers, the hand ever stretched out to our weakness and helplessness, and the riches in glory in Christ that are always sufficient. Over the whole event of the fire and its aftermath one Bible verse matched the situation again and again: 'God meant it' (Genesis 50:20).

Yes, and there was more that he 'meant', for by his planning and intention, St. Leonard's was already equipped with all those people who figure in the account – named and unnamed ones whose talents, commitment and giving were there at the Lord's disposal when his moment 'struck'. John tells their story faithfully. But, as you might expect, he fails to mention the one piece of divine forethought which, to me at any rate (and I won't be alone), stands in the foreground of the Lord's wise thinking ahead. He had already brought John Skinner to be your Rector, and who better – indeed, who anything like as well – to take the helm at such a time as that?

May you, like me, be lifted up in God by this narrative! May your eyes too brim with the tears that so often accompany heartfelt worship and some fresh awareness of how great Jesus is and how precious his loving care!

Alec Motyer
Poynton 2006

A typical Victorian Church interior, dark and formal
I(A)

An attractive setting alongside a main route into the city Centre

The 145 foot spire can be seen for miles around

The inflexible layout of the chancel, when church choirs predominated

II(A)

Top: Most of these finely carved choir stalls are relocated under the West-Window

Top right: This fine pulpit gave the preacher a excellent view, but for some of the congregation at least, severe neck strain

Bottom right: These memorial doors, badly scarred by the fire, were in memory of Clive Chesterfield OBE, a youth leader in the '50's'

III(A)

*Sheila Goldswain surveying
her tiny charges*

One end of the small Foyer, used for the expanding crèche

*A general view after a morning service: see how small the all
purpose Foyer was!*
IV(A)

The Church Hall in Roberts Road, at the heart of the estate

The foundation stone laid in 1889

The popular Holiday Club, as well as the regular Children's Groups on Sundays met here

V(A)

The interior of the hall was depressingly dark, and valiant efforts were made to brighten it up. It is still in full use, by the Community as well as the Church

Mary Banks and Graham and Joy Ireland, our superb crèche leader. Graham was a Boy Juco Leader. Mary was a Girl Juco Leader for many years and latterly led the Covie Group with her husband David

Central Middle Schoool, slightly nearer to the church was used by our Adventurers for a short while, led by Gordon Rice (right)

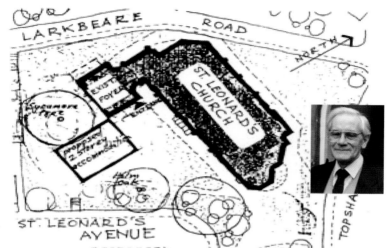

Above: Early sketch plans for extra accommodation, the sycamore (from left) and the two Holm Oaks were protected trees Below: A more advanced plan alongside St Leonard's Avenue. Inset: Alan Anderson, our first Architect

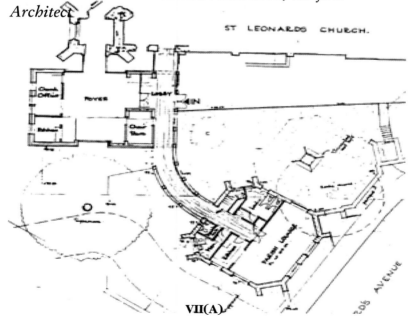

VII(A)

George Bevington
Rector from 1960-83
With his wife Eileen
(right)

Keith Lockhart, a highly respec-
ted local GP (left), John Skinner
(centre), Graham Tomlin
Curate from 1986-89

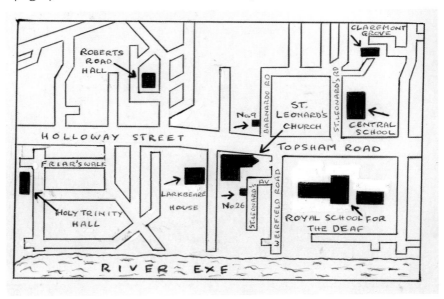

Introduction

The fire at St. Leonard's, on the night of August 23rd 1989, had such far reaching consequences - and I mean consequences for good - that we can, with full justification, exclaim "Thank God for the fire!". Even now, some 17 years on, it is hard to believe that so much was achieved through so little – just one match!

Through it, God chose to bring about a significant transformation of both people and buildings, in order to fast-forward the work of the Gospel, not just in the remaining years of the 90's, but on into the 21st Century. It is as significant as that!

What did it produce? In terms of buildings, a superb new Church Centre, seamlessly integrated with a beautifully refurbished and modernised Victorian church. In terms of people, a church family tested and renewed, made ready to meet the ever greater opportunities ahead.

For all of us, it was a huge privilege to have lived through this very special time, and it has certainly left its mark on us for good. God was powerfully and visibly at work. It was a deeply humbling experience to know that He wanted to use people like us in this new and exciting advance for the Gospel!

Outreach is nothing new at St. Leonard's. It has been an integral part of church life over many years as new opportunities and challenges have arisen, especially locally, as the parish has grown numerically. Large, grand mansions (1) which were once a distinctive feature, were pulled down and replaced by tightly knit housing estates. One of these was in the Roberts Road area. How did the church members respond to this new development just down the hill? Under the dynamic leadership of their new Rector, aged 25 (2), the youngest in the Church of England at the time, they caught the vision of outreach to those newcomers. They built a brand new hall right in the heart of this new community, so that new families would not even have to trek 'up the hill' (as older residents used to say) to the church. They and their children could just go along the road to hear about the Christian faith, in a nearby hall, without the danger of crossing the increasingly busy Topsham Road. What could be easier? The church members drew up detailed, plans and then laid the Hall Foundation Stone on August 24, 1889 (3). Would you believe it - this was 100 years (less one day) before the most recent fire!

Undoubtedly these new premises were less daunting for any previously unchurched newcomers. But how far was it possible to integrate them with what was already going on up at the church? We shall never know. Maybe it created a cultural divide which proved too big for some to cross.

On this particular point the writer of a recent article in the church press challenged his readers to look critically at their own church premises. "How would tentative newcomers from today's culture," he wrote, "view your church? When did you last take a good, critical look at the physical environment of your church? The interior of a church ought to be welcoming, comfortable and conducive to worship. Yet over the years the church buildings can easily become jaded and even 'scuffed'. To a visitor or a potential new member or new regular worshipper, the facilities of a church – often installed to suit the tastes of an earlier, less-sophisticated era might seem quite primitive or unacceptably antiquated. Churches vary enormously in style, of course, both across and within the denominations, but the broad aim of all is to be a holy place, as befits God's house. In an era of declining church attendances overall, it is now particularly important to make our churches look inviting. After all, the first-time visitor is likely to be used to all the comforts of the secular world, both in private living quarters and in public venues such as shopping centres, cinemas, theatres and even offices…To enter a church that is cold, a bit scruffy and somehow unloved in appearance or needlessly at odds with present-day expectations is off-putting. Such an appearance sends out the wrong signals – it speaks of a church in decline even where that might not actually be the case." (4)

Now whether every detail accurately describes St. Leonard's is irrelevant. What is remarkable is that, at a stroke, the fire accomplished most, if not all, of those transformations described! It is beyond dispute that the church interior was dark and drab, uncomfortable and unwelcoming, inflexible and cramped, not least for the Crèche in the Foyer. Faithful church members had probably grown so used to it over the years that they failed to realise just how off-putting and dated it was to newcomers. Visitors would gain an impression of a Christian Community, apparently contentedly living in the past, largely out of touch with the huge changes taking place all around them.

The spiritual life was clearly there, but not perhaps the willingness to change in order to make things more relevant to newcomers - not least for those with little or no church background, of whom there were to be a growing number.

The fire set in motion a sequence of events which was to result in an amazing transformation creating a magnificent launch-pad for outreach into the new Millennium. This is the remarkable story of how it happened.

So who is this being written for?

It is written, in the first place, as a vivid reminder to all those who were privileged to be church members through those formative years. Most of their names are woven into the large colourful tapestry, produced by Anita Beasley and her gifted team that now hangs in the Entrance Hall (5). These are the ones (young and old) who faced the tests and challenges. God took us - together with all our strengths and weaknesses. He gradually, and sometimes fairly painfully, transformed us by His love and grace. For us it is a hugely encouraging experience to look back upon!

Then secondly, it is recorded for the stimulus and benefit of newcomers, some of whom perhaps have never fully realised the remarkable heritage they have entered into by joining St. Leonard's. Reflecting on what God has done, their vision of the future will hopefully be stronger, and they will, even more eagerly, want others to be reached with the Gospel.

Thirdly, it may encourage visitors belonging to other churches, who long to seize their own opportunities in their situations (without the help of the fire, of course!), so that they too will be used for effective outreach in the 21st Century.

Fourthly, and most importantly, it is written that God, who made it all happen, gets the glory! He knew just what needed doing at St. Leonard's. He knew what obstacles had to be removed. He knew how to transform his people to fit them for witness in a rapidly-changing world. His 'fingerprints' were on everything!

Finally, I wish to express my great gratitude to Gordon Rice, Churchwarden at the time of the fire. He has kindly contributed so many detailed footnotes for this story. For he was the Chairman of the Building Group during the whole of those 10 years - and a hands-on Chairman at that! Without his enormous energy, total commitment, amazing grasp of detail and dogged perseverance, it is doubtful if, humanly speaking, the end result would ever have been achieved. Clearly, he was God's man for the moment!

My grateful thanks also go to David Banks, Gordon's fellow Warden and Youth Leader, who first encouraged me to write this story and for his enthusiasm and expert help in preparing for its publication. Last but by no means least, to Margaret Unsworth, ably supported by Spencer and the family, who somehow managed to cope with the running of the busy Church Office (leading the Admin.Team) (6) through this demanding and disruptive time. To Margaret everyone mattered equally. Whoever they were (casual visitor, workman, troubled church member) - and despite the bustle of activity all around - she welcomed them. This was all a natural part of her service for the Lord. Her extraordinary practical efficiency, patience and spiritual attitude were an example to all - and now she has also kindly produced this type-script. Very grateful thanks!

Additional Note When this manuscript was nearing completion, I happened to have a rather remarkable conversation with Tina Smith, who was Church Treasurer from 1989-94, almost exactly coinciding with the dates of the fire and its aftermath.

We met at the reception after Tom Davis's funeral on December 10th, 04, when our thoughts turned, quite naturally, to the way God had used Tom so greatly throughout this project. Tina was recalling such vivid and detailed memories of all that had happened behind the scenes that I asked her if she would write these down for me to enhance the story. This she readily agreed to do, and the result (in full) is included as a special appendix.

This is both fascinating and exciting and gives further glory to God. My very grateful thanks to you, Tina, for sharing your "Treasurer's Perspective" with us!

Inevitably, hundreds of people are not mentioned in this story even though their contribution (under God) was significant. Our indebtedness extends to them as well as those whose names are included. However I must mention my wife, Marilyn, whose invaluable ministry of encouragement has acted as a catalyst to so many, and (of course) extends far beyond the confines of this story, yet was of particular importance during these testing but memorable years.

I was particularly pleased when Alec Motyer agreed to write the Foreward for this story. He has had such a close association with St. Leonard's for so many years, and he has also been a close personal friend for even longer. As befits someone who is co-editor (with John Stott) of the valued IVP Bible Speaks Today Commentary Series, his visits to us were always relevant and inspiring. How privileged we were to sit at the feet of someone who not only expounded the Scriptures so ably but did so with such evident delight!

So thank you, Alec! We are greatly indebted to you not only for this particular contribution, but also for all the other aspects of your enlightening and encouraging ministry to us at St. Leonard's. We thank God for you.

Chapter One

The prelude to the fire

So why was the fire so significant? It was mainly because of the years of frustration that preceded it. What was the cause of this growing frustration? Two conflicting things. Steady church growth (of a numerical kind) on the one hand, and totally inadequate premises to cope with it on the other. Clearly the trend itself was most welcome and greatly encouraging! Any church would surely be delighted to be faced with it! But the inability to cope with it, through factors entirely beyond the church's control, was to prove most discouraging. That was the nub of the frustration.

So what was this specific area of growth? It was what to do with the number of new children, especially of Crèche age, who were being brought by their parents. For their older children, there was no major problem, except that of being some distance away from their parents across the busy Topsham Road, a quarter of a mile away down in Roberts Road. See map on page VIII(A). Practically all our lively children's groups, led by a superb team of dedicated leaders (1) met in the roomy (if now very old-fashioned) Church Hall in Roberts Road (2). At least there was room for some expansion there, however inadequate the accommodation was in other ways. But all we had for babies and

and tiny children, who needed to be near or with their parents, was a small section of the old tiny Foyer with no baby changing facilities (3). Built some 20 years earlier, as a multi-purpose extension (4), it could only cope with limited numbers at the far end, safely away from the busy entrance. A few extra newcomers could be squeezed in but a steady influx caused problems, not least on wet days when pushchairs (and large prams in those days!) had to be brought in under cover (5).

It became apparent to the Church Council that something just had to be done, and with some urgency. The concerned parents needed to know, as well as the rest of the Church, that steps were being taken to solve the problem. After all, our whole object was to welcome newcomers, not deter them!

At an early stage, the PCC set up a working group (6), chaired by Gordon Rice, who himself led the Adventurers Group for 7-10's in Roberts Road Hall on Sunday mornings. Another key person on the group was Joy Ireland (7), who organised the Crèche (8), and we were fortunate in having several other members with building expertise available to help. They were all fully aware of the needs, and with the prayers of the congregation behind them, they set about looking at all the various options (9). The first of these was hiring temporary Portakabins, similar to the ones used by contractors. They could be sited next to or near the Foyer, to provide some overflow space. They were expensive and hardly ideal with their steps up to the entrance but they could have provided some much-needed respite in the circumstances. In our desperation we were unaware at first that even temporary structures like Portakabins might need planning permission.

This was to be our first contact with the Planning Authorities, who were suddenly made aware of stirrings at St. Leonard's! This required them to re-visit some of their old files from 20 years previously and (unknown to us at the time) uncover some of their former concerns over the style of the old Foyer. Their view? No way would Portakabins (even temporary ones) be allowed. That much was quite definite!

Knowing little of what was in their file from the past, we searched for other longer-term options. We engaged an Architect, Alan Anderson from Bridgwater (10), who drew up detailed plan after plan - five altogether - for small premises in different parts of the Churchyard (well away from the Foyer) and including the allotment area alongside Larkbeare Road. All these proposals were turned down, partly because most would involve felling some of the trees, which all had preservation orders on them (11). The surrounds of the Church were, we gathered, in a highly sensitive area environmentally. Any proposed premises had to allow for considerable growth-space for each of the trees - which in practical terms left no remaining room at all! Whichever way we turned, the Planners appeared unyielding - there seemed no possible way out – it was almost becoming farcical. The patience of the Building Group and Architect - let alone the PCC and the whole congregation - was being sorely tried. All our best efforts were apparently being thwarted (12).

We were all deeply puzzled as we continued to cry to God for some viable way forward. "Surely there must be some solution somewhere? Have we really considered every alternative?" "Please, Lord, intervene in some way."

And He did! It was just then that the arsonist struck - and that one match altered everything - literally! - as we were to appreciate more fully later on. God had heard our cry. God did understand the problem. He already knew both the short-term and the long-term needs of the future. He had used this run-up time to test our faith, patience and resolve to the limit, but then came the fire and with it a new direction under God's providential hand (13).

To quote Churchill's famous dictum (in rather different circumstances, it has to be admitted!) "This was not the end. This was not the beginning of the end, but it was the end of the beginning". For us, it certainly was. But there were (unknown to us) even bigger challenges and tests yet to come.

Chapter Two

The night of the fire

It was in the early hours of Wednesday morning, about 1.30am on August 23rd 1989, that the unknown arsonist struck. A local resident in St. Leonard's Avenue (1) first raised the alarm, and the Fire Brigade were on the scene in no time. Clearly this was a major incident, and their blaring sirens woke the whole neighbourhood. Out of their windows local people could see for themselves the flames leaping high in the sky and the thick pall of smoke. It was all very dramatic!

We have always been grateful to have friendly neighbours around the church, and we thanked God that one of them was still awake that early in the morning to ring for urgent help. We also thanked God that the Fire Service responded so promptly to avert much more wide-spread damage.

The fire was actually started in the Foyer, possibly by someone sleeping rough in the small covered porch. Once the Foyer was ablaze, the church tower began to act as a giant flue, drawing enormous heat and thick smoke into the church interior (2). The whole church was filled with choking smoke from top to bottom, and smoke was billowing out of the top clerestory windows, making them look like a line of ships' funnels!

Later on, with hindsight, we were able to see that the Fire Brigade had brought the fire under control at a crucial moment (3). The Foyer (our immediate problem) had been completely destroyed, but the church itself, while being severely smoke-damaged, was nevertheless structurally intact. They had prevented the fire from doing far worse damage, which at that point it was certainly threatening to do. With an eye to the future, it was to be a most significant moment. For our part, of course, we didn't realise it - but quite clearly God did.

The next morning, those in the neighbourhood were in a state of shock and disbelief, "How could anyone do such a wicked thing - and to a church too!" It was specially outrageous, in their view, that a church of all places, should not be under divine protection and therefore immune! To all of us, it was indeed a sorry sight, with the burnt-out shell and the smouldering remains. Inside the church, the entrance doors were badly scorched and every conceivable surface was covered by a sticky black residue left by the smoke. Nothing was spared - walls, ceiling, windows, organ pipes, font, pulpit, choir stalls, pews, chairs, Bibles, banners (4), hymn books - everything! You couldn't touch anything without getting sticky and dirty. It was chaotic! (5)

Sadly, a funeral service (6) arranged for that afternoon had to be rapidly transferred elsewhere and the mourners informed, but the very first church meeting after the fire was a Prayer meeting. How appropriate! The one thing we all instinctively wanted to do was to talk corporately to our loving heavenly Father about what had just happened, and to seek His mind for the days ahead. As someone has said, "We didn't know what the future held, but we knew who held the future." It was all in His capable hands. As the hymn says, 'What a privilege to carry everything to God in prayer'. It was very definitely so for those who met together that Wednesday night.

God certainly led us as to what to do the next Sunday. Should we find another venue for our Services or should we try to get even the minimum cleaned in time? It was a mammoth and daunting task for such a huge building, but surprisingly, a professional cleaning firm (7), with all the necessary high-powered equipment, the appropriate detergents and an extremely energetic staff, were free and willing to drop everything else and come to our aid. It was a remarkable provision and a very close call. They started on Thursday and finished late on Friday night! It was a whirlwind 2 days. Everything from the floor to 8 feet up on the walls had been thoroughly cleaned - so that hopefully no one who came on Sunday would get dirty, nor would they mind the lingering smell of detergent and smoke.

With everything around the burnt-out Foyer now sealed off, the only way into the church was through the narrow East end entrance. The congregation poured in for the main services, both of which were most memorable. Apart from amazement at being able to meet in the church at all, there was deep gratitude and joy that things had not been a lot worse, despite the extent of the damage. The words of the first hymn seemed to catch the mood perfectly : 'Tell out my soul the greatness of the Lord! Unnumbered blessings give my spirit voice....in God my Saviour shall my heart rejoice'. There was a similar response in the evening as we sang 'How great Thou art!' before turning to the Bible, to see what being 'tested by fire' really meant for us as Christian people. (8)

Throughout the day, there was no sense of dismay or self-pity, but rather deep peace and renewed commitment. We knew that God could use what had happened for good - and for His glory. But just what He had in store for us none of us knew.

Chapter Three

New beginnings

Changes now came thick and fast! The most urgent needs were for those children's groups that had suddenly become homeless as a result of the fire - the Crèche, obviously, but also the Girl Juco Group, who had previously met in a room high up in the tower. Where could these children now meet the following Sunday?

For the 12-15 babies in the Crèche, Peter and Ginny Hocking, who lived across in Barnardo Road, immediately came to our rescue by opening their home. What a generous offer this was - and so near too! But what about the mobile toddlers who clearly needed more space? A similar generous offer came from Hywel Jones, the Head of the Royal School for the Deaf (1), our neighbour along Topsham Road, who put at our disposal the specialist premises at the school for their smaller children. These facilities were so well equipped with large toys and apparatus that they soon became quite a popular draw for new children, even though they were located at the far end of the school, nearly opposite Matford Lane. But not only did Hywel help us with a new home for this age-group, he offered a room for the Girl Jucos as well. This lively group of 10-12's, led by Graham and Hilary Dixon, were feeling particularly deprived at having lost their special den, so secret and exclusive in the church tower, and approached by a spiral staircase! They used to love meeting there - and bringing new friends along to see it. They came to appreciate their modern room in the school, and all the extra space, but they still felt nostalgic at having to leave the seclusion of their den so suddenly.

Later, when the church was being refurbished, we had even more reason to be grateful to Hywel Jones for his generosity and welcome, but these first offers from the Hockings and the Jones' (Sandra as well!) - who were all active church members - were most timely and greatly appreciated. We thanked God for them.

The next huge change was for the Building Group (2) , who now had a completely new agenda and Authority to work under. All previous plans for outside extensions were now shelved, to concentrate on restoring the interior of the church as their top priority. It was also something of a relief to work under the Church Authorities (the Diocesan Advisory Committee), rather than the City Planning Authorities, for hopefully they would have a rather more positive and sympathetic attitude. Now, of course, there was absolutely no argument about whether something could/should be done or not. Something definitely had to be done to restore the church. It all helped to concentrate the minds of the PCC and the Building Group!

Clearly big issues lay ahead. Should the church just be restored as it was before the fire - the total cost being met by Insurance - or should other more radical options be considered? What about re-ordering and modernising the church completely which would of course necessitate raising the extra money ourselves? It seemed too good an opportunity to be missed - could this become part of God's plan to update St. Leonard's for a new era of outreach? Suddenly there were new horizons ahead, with plenty of scope for imaginative, yet sensitive and responsible, action. It was quite a challenging, liberating and heady experience as we worked through the various possibilities before us. These were, indeed, exciting times that God had given us - and all so totally unexpected!

We consulted the Diocesan Advisory Committee (who have to approve all church alterations) at an early stage, to gauge their response to our thinking. The DAC Chairman, Archdeacon John Richards (3) paid us a visit and started making some even more radical suggestions than we had ever dared to consider. We were quite taken aback and greatly heartened by his enthusiasm. We now hoped that our plans would get a very sympathetic hearing and probable approval. How different to our previous experience with the Civic Authorities!

One key decision taken at this early stage was to have very beneficial and unforeseen consequences when the Centre was finally built - still a long way off at that stage, of course. It was to have a completely new entrance cut into the side of the church, to bypass the tower and to avoid the congestion that used to build up at the back of the church, partly due to the positioning of the large font. This decision not only made good sense for the church building itself, but was also going to prove pivotal in relation to access from the new Church Centre. In a remarkable way, it was going to be a means of unifying the eventual premises, enabling us to move seamlessly from one area to the other. Clearly God, knowing our future needs, led us in this key decision, long before any plans were drawn up for the Centre. Another key provision was the offer of help from the Cathedral, whose stonemasons were able to make the new doorway blend so superbly. In fact it is difficult today to realise that this was not a part of the original design.

When all our plans (4) were drawn up and fully approved by the DAC, we were then, of course, eager to know how much it would cost, over and above any insurance monies (5). We went out to tender, and H. E. Hansford & Son of Honiton were the best firm for the work. Now, at long last, we had our target figure, which seemed rather daunting. However, the whole Church Family agreed that this was a very special opportunity to do something really significant and lasting for the future, and the majority were prepared to face the huge challenge ahead. They went to work with a will. The first of a series of Prayer and Pledge weekends was fixed, most appropriately, for the Sunday before Easter. What better time to face the prospect of sacrificial giving! The key prayer day on the Saturday enabled as many of the congregation as possible to come to the Church to seek God's guidance. It was well organised by David and Tina Smith, Lay Reader (6) and Treasurer respectively, and it was a great encouragement to everyone to see how many were able to participate. Clearly God was stirring people's heart's to respond willingly and generously (7). It was even more encouraging to see the large bowl in the middle of the centre aisle, visibly filled to overflowing with pledges the following day. A great start had been made.

There were some who were less able to give financially than others, but nevertheless they were still eager to offer gifts of other kinds. One such was David Griffiths from West Grove Road, one of our gifted team of musicians. He formed a special music group, 'The Flaming Tongues'(8), who sold copies of a cassette tape they recorded and arranged special concerts to raise funds. Others too had imaginative ways of taking part, not least members of the Contact Group (the 15's-18's) who raised money through car washes on Saturday mornings in the church car park. One of the young paperboys contributed some money from his round. It was all intensely moving to see everyone, young and old alike, eager to be involved in some way.

During the 14 months before the refurbishment began, there were, of course, a number of Weddings, and special efforts had to be made to try and brighten up the blackened church for these happy occasions. The first one on September 2nd, after the fire, was also special and unusual for other reasons, for both bride and groom were totally deaf. Heather Hurd, who lived just down the road from the church and Tony Barkworth had met as fellow pupils at the School for the Deaf. They were prepared for their marriage by Graham Tomlin (9) before he completed his Curacy to move to Oxford, and the Chaplain for the Deaf Community in Devon, George Firth (10), did sign language throughout the Service, not least for the Wedding Vows, when bride and groom had to respond in sign language themselves. It was a most memorable occasion for all concerned!

Then, for two further Weddings the following Easter (11), another effort to brighten up the drab church involved buying specially a long off-cut of carpet for the centre aisle. Coming through the narrow East End door (like everyone else) the bride and her attendants then walked right down the side aisle before coming up the centre aisle and vice versa on the way out. Everyone had a perfect view, one way or the other. Apart from this double bonus, the only hazard was avoiding getting the bride's heels stuck in the grating on the way round down the side aisle.

When Hansford's, under their Works Manager, Brian Sandercock, started work on the church interior on October 1st 1990, we were able to move to the Royal School for the Deaf for our Sunday Services. What an important experience this was going to prove to be - for it suddenly provided a heady taster for the distant future, still nearly 4 years away. But what had God got in store for us now?

Chapter Four

A temporary lodging-place

How thankful we were to be able to hold our Services just along Topsham Road! There was, of course, plenty of parking around the School for the Deaf and also no new-comers would get lost trying to find it. It was a wonderful provision. Not only were we able to use the large colour-ful assembly hall, but we also had free use of the dining hall and excellent kitchen facilities and some of the smaller ancillary rooms as well. It was a truly liberating experience in that we could now do things, under one roof, that had not previously been possible - such as after-service refreshments for all, meals together, socials and parties, which greatly enhanced our fellowship.

Whole families were together for the first time for infor-mal occasions. It gave us a new dimension as a Church Family, though it took us a little while to adjust to all the exciting new possibilities now open to us. It was a novel experience!

There were also one or two minor revolutions - of the best possible kind - not least for those regulars who came to the 8 o'clock Communion Service, who were very set in their traditional ways, for we now met together in one of the smaller seminar rooms. This was something of a cultural shock for those who came. In those days, the dozen or so who came were used to sitting as far away as possible from each other in different far-flung corners of the church, hardly communicating with each other either before or afterwards! How unbelievably depressing it was, not least for the clergy leading the service, what a strange way to start a Sunday - and above all what an abuse of the Lord's Supper! Suddenly everything was transformed as we met at the school around the Lord's Table, in a half circle in a fairly small room. What happened? Everyone actually greeted each other warmly as they came in, and stayed behind afterwards too! Only just enough chairs were put out, so that it was (much) closer fellowship. It proved such an important change, which everyone adapted to, that when we eventually returned to the church, we were determined not to revert to the bad old habits. From then onwards, we met in a circle in the Chancel for this service. This was just one of the many changes brought about by the fire.

The Deaf School Assembly Hall, which we used for our main services (1), was just about big enough for us to squeeze into, and it took the considerable and sustained time and effort of a willing team to set it ready and clear away each Saturday and Sunday night. We arranged the chairs sideways on, which not only gave a less formal atmosphere, but also enabled us to enjoy the huge jungle mural covering the whole of the back wall. What a magnificent sight it was, glorying in God's colourful creation! For the Christmas Services, every part of the big platform was also packed, we were able to offer mince pies to our many guests afterwards, and during these 4 months the church grew steadily. We were all enjoying this novel, unrestricted experience so much, that we knew it would be quite hard to leave when the time eventually came - however great the attraction of a newly refurbished church!

Meanwhile the work of restoration was going ahead

steadily. By far the biggest job was the thorough scrubbing of the church from top to bottom. It was quite hazardous, having to use the tallest mobile scaffolding towers to reach the highest corners - but thankfully no accidents occurred. Some of the scorch marks on the stonework were particularly hard to remove, and the inside of the tower was really badly affected. Once roof and walls were clean, then the rest of the work could begin in earnest.

A delightful incident took place one day, during the workmen's lunch break, witnessed by them in total silence. It was quite riveting. This was at a time when the church floor was strewn with tools, cables, equipment of one sort or another and assorted building debris everywhere, including the heavy grills which normally cover the heating ducts. It was all fairly chaotic as you would expect - and quite dangerous. For safety reasons, no unauthorized people were allowed in the church and hard hats had to be worn by everyone. Suddenly the workmen heard a click of the side door being opened and they watched (in total silence) as an elderly lady entered as if she knew her way around. She was obviously looking for something special and walked slowly up and down the open heating ducts, stopping now and then and peering in. This was of course before they had been cleaned and they were filled with accumulated dust and dirt and assorted cables alongside the large water pipes. Then suddenly she stopped, stooped down low and reached for a tiny shining object in one of the ducts. She straightened up and held it up in triumph! She had found it! A precious ring that had been lost through the grating many years previously at an 8 o'clock Communion Service, which she and her elderly sister attended regularly. What joy! Clutching it tightly she picked her way back to the entrance and left as quietly as she had entered. And no-one moved or made a sound! They were all dumbstruck by what they saw, fearing an accident if they disturbed her. As far as she was concerned, she was totally unaware of being observed! What a wonderful reminder of Jesus' parable of the lost coin! (2)

One of the important aspects of the refurbishment was not only the installation of a vastly improved lighting system, but also a carefully co-ordinated colour scheme throughout. This is where God provided just the right person to help us, for our architect confessed to being less than an expert in this area. Imagine our surprise, then, to be offered, free of charge, expert professional advice from someone who was working on the re-building of the Royal Devon and Exeter Hospital in Barrack Road. The Managing Director of the Bristol firm of architects doing the work, offered his chief colour consultant, Marion Gardiner, to help us! (3) One of her specialist skills was doing colour schemes on the grand scale, and although she had not had previous experience of church interiors, she studied our plans, and spent some considerable time just sitting in the middle of the church, amidst the chaos, while work was going on all around her, soaking in her surroundings. We were so grateful for the great care she took and more than impressed with the results she produced for the long drapes either side of the chancel, the curtains, chairs and carpets. She got it exactly right in every detail, creating such a superb atmosphere for worship at St. Leonard's, which has been so much admired ever since!

The choice of chairs was very democratic: Four sample chairs were chosen from the leading ecclesiastical suppliers, and a test session arranged after the main services one Sunday when people could cast their vote for the style and colour of their choice. A procession of people solemnly sampled each one in turn (like a sequence of the old T.V. programme 'Candid Camera') and the eventual result was overwhelmingly in favour of one of them the ones you see now.   It was all quite fun. Every-one seemed to appreciate being involved. (4)

Although we were greatly looking forward to returning to the church - so beautifully transformed - it was neverthe-less tinged with sadness. We had really enjoyed our 4 months at the school, appreciated the hospitality given to us and benefited from the change. It was our very first taste of bright, modern Sundays, extra space, splendid facilities and also all-age family fellowship. We had actually caught a passing glimpse of what things could be like in the future, - not least the way <u>worship</u> was enhanced by our experience at the school - and in relation to our witness to the newcomer. Unknown to us at that time, it would take a further 3 1/2 years for this dream to be fulfilled, but God had allowed us to taste what he had in store.

One thing was certain and so assuring: while we had been meeting at the school, God had continued to be power-fully at work amongst us and we had been drawn closer to Him.   We knew that while special church buildings undoubtedly have their place for Christians to meet in, they are not absolutely essential. God had graciously met with us as He had promised; for Jesus had said, "Where two or three are gathered together in my name, there I am in the midst of them" (5) . That, we knew, was gloriously true!

The dramatic fire lit up the night sky at 1 am

The tower entrance from the burning Foyer took the brunt of the smoke, and was extremely resistant to cleaning

The fire is thought to have been started at the left hand end in a small alcove for prams

The blackened interior of the Church, affecting every surface

Looking towards the Chancel, with a roll of carpet specially bought for two of the subsequent weddings, to brighten things up!

II(B)

Alan and Gaynor Stevens. Alan had just arrived as Curate (after Graham Tomlin) was first on the scene of the fire

Ben Harris, thrown in the deep end as our very first lay assistant

St Leonard (left) is the patron saint of prisoners, looking thoroughly cleaned up after being totally blackened

A picture, taken by an Express & Echo Photographer on the first Sunday after the fire and after the minimum of cleaning

With the Foyer gutted, the congregation came into the
Church by the South side entrance

Our neighbours, the Royal School for the Deaf, came to
our aid immediately for some of our activities

The crèche was transferred to 9 Barnardo Road.
Topsham Road is just beyond the red car
V(B)

The first task was to scrub the Church from top to bottom

The floor tiles were removed, and the sunken heating ducts were all cleaned out

VI(B)

A group of our lively Jucos going off to a Whitsun camp on Dartmoor

The Deaf School Assembly Hall, where we held our services during the refurbishment, having a stunningly beautiful Jungle mural covering the whole of one wall
Inset: Gill Behenna was the outstanding Chaplain both for the Royal School for the Deaf and the Devon Deaf Community

The site cleared in time for Easter. Note the three crosses.
After death there was to be resurrection. Below, the
new entrance in the expert hands of stone masons from
the Cathedral

Chapter Five

Coming home again

The final week, leading up to that first Sunday back, January 27th 1991, was quite hectic. There was still much to be done after the Contractors had finished, for the carpeting had to be laid and vacuumed, the huge drapes to be hung, 390 chairs put in place and books to be put out. There was a wonderfully willing team of helpers, and great excitement was in the air. All was now ready for the services the following day!

It is hard to describe accurately the atmosphere as people poured in next day through the new entrance. As people sat down and started to take in their new surroundings, there was a stunned silence for several minutes before conversations began. It was overwhelming - and such a total contrast to their last memories of the church interior! The beautiful combination of colours, the superb lighting (1) the new church furnishings - especially the crafted communion rail - the sense of space in the chancel, comfortable chairs - it was almost too good to be true! The carpet gave a new dimension of width and warmth, the lighting on the ceiling a new sense of brightness and height, and the spotlights on the central cross, a perfect centrepiece. Interestingly enough, the carpet proved an immediate invitation for small children to sit down on it - anywhere. They seemed immediately to feel at home! It also enhanced the sound quality, contrary to some predictions, and greatly aided our concentration by cutting out extraneous and distracting noises. Groups like visiting choirs enjoyed coming to St. Leonard's for their concerts, not only for the excellent acoustics but also because of the standard of comfort for their audience. It proved a most attractive setting and there was no shortage of book-ings!

The flexibility of all the church furnishings was a consider-able new advantage, not only on Sundays, but for versatile weekday use as well. The Maundy Thursday Communion Service, for instance, could have seating arranged around the Lord's Table. The Holiday Club could have a clear central area. Our two local church schools (Central First and Middle) could rearrange the seating most suitably for each occasion. Drama companies (like 'Riding Lights') (2) could stage their productions in the round if they wished. There was no end to the possible permutations and imaginative layouts - and it was a great joy to have all these new freedoms available.

Needless to say, both the services on that opening Sunday were times of great rejoicing and gratitude to God! 'Praise my soul the King of heaven, to his feet thy tribute bring' echoed around the church, before we focussed on Jacob's overwhelming encounter with God from Genesis 28: 'How awesome is this place! This is none other than the house of God; this is the gate of heaven'. At the evening Communion Service our focus was on the immense privi-lege of being like 'living stones, being built into a spiritual house to be a holy priesthood offering spiritual sacrifices acceptable to God through Jesus Christ' (1.Peter 2:5) and called to 'declare the praises of him who called us out of darkness into his marvellous light'.

In the coming weeks, we welcomed many visitors, not least members of Church PCCs (from near and far), who were trying to adapt and modernise their own church premises. Some even asked us for the name and address of our arsonist! Others who came for Weddings and Funerals were pleasantly surprised to find a church so welcoming and comfortable. One elderly lady had even brought her own cushion, anticipating the usual hard Anglican seat! Before we opened our mouths the premises themselves were conveying a powerful message: 'Please stay as long as you can' and a great many did just that. Especially after the evening services, for example, many people lingered around for an hour or more, including a number coming from a local 'battered wives' refuge, even without refreshments to offer them, for at that stage, we only had a tiny temporary kitchenette at the base of the tower. These after-service times were in fact among the most fruitful times spiritually when people were most open to God, as they reflected on what they had heard him saying through his Word, the Bible, and shared their concerns.

It was obviously important to keep everything spick and span, and an excellent cleaning team (3) was mobilised, led by Sarah Pritchard, Head of our Central First School. One immediate problem they had to contend with was the inevitable dirt brought in by hundreds of people coming through the newly cut entrance, with no porch or mats outside! Furthermore when it was wet and windy, the prevailing westerly winds blew straight into the church, and brought everything with them - leaves, dirt and all! The willing team had many hazards to contend with, and the purchase of an industrial cleaner made all the difference. With no lobby space for wet clothes either, we realised just how blest we had been with all the extensive facilities (4) at the School for the Deaf. It was quite a sharp learning curve for everyone! Perhaps it is worth mentioning at this point that the cleaning of the organ had to be left until all the main refurbishment had been completed, not least because of the dust. It was a long, specialist job, carried out by our usual maintenance firm, which involved dismantling and thoroughly cleaning every individual piece. This work was entirely covered by insurance (5). We took the opportunity of asking the firm to lower the pitch to coincide with the piano so that both instruments could, on occasions, be played together. This also had the added advantage of enhancing congregational worship, which is such a feature at St. Leonard's, by enabling men to reach most of the higher notes. For them it made all the difference!

Alongside the church one eyesore remained, and was still in full view of everyone as they approached the church. It was the burnt-out shell of the old Foyer, which had to some extent, at least, been screened off by shrubs and flowers - but it still looked awful, to put it mildly! So a team of men, led by Bryan Power and Richard Dickinson, decided to do something about it. They completely demolished it, carrying away loads of rubble and trying to preserve anything that might be useful in the future (6). It was so significant that they successfully completed the work just before Easter (7), erecting three large crosses made from re-claimed wood on the cleared site, which of course proved a powerful visual-aid for all the Easter worshippers of new life and hope in Christ arising from death and destruction. What a symbolic inspiration for all of us as we looked to God for the future!

Chapter Six

The new Church Centre

At long last, with the clearing of the site where the old Foyer had once been, we felt that there was a new start - the past was now behind us. But what now? What will we be allowed to put up in its place? We were very conscious that once again we were back under the authority of the City Planners and because of the extreme sensitivity of the site environmentally, they would view any plans with special caution.

As our discussions with the Planners resumed, we became more fully aware of the real reasons behind their opposition to all our previous proposals. It emerged that they had had an intense dislike of the original design of the old Foyer, and had been greatly embarrassed that their predecessors at the time had ever given approval for it. To them it was an eyesore. It was in their words 'a brutal modern extension'[1] which disfigured the site. The fire, therefore, and the complete destruction of the Foyer through it, came as an undisguised relief to them! A blot on the landscape had mercifully been removed. Now at last they were very willing to consider a suitable replacement. It must of course be of the very highest quality in their opinion and in keeping with the surroundings.

Now with possible permission in sight, for the right design, what sort of Church Centre [2] would be needed not just for the immediate present but for future needs as well – if no further extension would be allowed? This time round there would be little financial help. We would be faced with a far, far greater challenge in raising practically all the money ourselves. Fortunately, perhaps, we were not to realise at that stage, that it would be a further 3 years before the Church Centre would finally be ready.

The first priority in all those early discussions was what had always been uppermost from the outset - namely catering for the needs of families with young children, who needed to be with or near their parents, especially newcomers and visitors. At the time we had over 220 children and young people in our groups. How many of these could we expect to cater for in our new premises (3) - and (most importantly) what provision should be made for further church growth?

The next key question was equally important. What about weekday use? To spend so much money, and to have fantastic facilities for children and young people for Sunday use only would hardly be good stewardship, if it remained an empty shell during the rest of the week. It must also be a multi-purpose Centre, well used every day of the week, for it to be really justified. How far were we able to anticipate that it would not only be increasingly used for a large number of 'church family' activities, but in demand too by outside bodies, Christian and secular, locally, regionally and occasionally nationally?

The PCC wrestled with these issues and convened congregational meetings to gauge a wider cross-section of viewpoint (4). Many hours were spent listening to one another, raising hard questions and contrary opinions, and 'speaking the truth in love' together. It proved a vital stage in the spiritual development of the whole church family. Here are some of the main arguments raised for prayer and consideration at the time:

First : <u>Missionary Giving</u>. "This Centre is going to cost a huge amount of money by any reckoning. How can it possibly be justified, when there are so many missionary needs? We give considerable sums - why couldn't we give a lot more, if we think extra money is available? How can we justify spending so much money on ourselves any-way?" These were powerful, searching questions, not to be brushed aside easily. The response followed two main lines. Would the missionaries actually benefit in practice by increased giving if the Church Centre wasn't built? Are we ourselves not just as much missionaries at home, as those called overseas, and shouldn't such a Church Centre enhance our own missionary outreach locally and then beyond?

Second : <u>Our own spiritual vitality.</u> Should we embark on such a huge project if our own spiritual condition together is not as deep and vibrant as it could/should be? Should we not first concentrate on getting ourselves into better spiritual shape, before embarking on any project of this nature? Surely that must be our greater priority? Again, the counter-argument was two-fold. If we wait for such an improvement in our spiritual state, which is a most laudable objective and one with which we would all agree, just how long should we wait, and how would we know when we were spiritually fit enough to begin? May not God want to use this particular project to stimulate further spiritual growth? Cannot the two go hand in hand, as we have already seen in a measure through the church refurbishment? Must it necessarily be either/or? Why not both/and?

Third : <u>"This seems a huge project just for our own benefit.</u> How can we justify spending all this money and effort, if the Church Centre will only be used for a small fraction of a week? Surely for most of the week, it would stand empty? Have we any idea who else might want to use it when we don't?" The response was again two-fold. "Obviously our church groups would have priority for its use, but there are plenty of outside groups who might well want to use such convenient premises as well as those within the deanery, diocese and national societies", and "with a growing church do we not want to plan for spare capacity so that we are not caught out again?"

These and other hard questions needed to be faced together, both to sharpen up our vision and to ensure appropriate realism. As people were prayerfully convinced of the rightness of this project, so they would be fully prepared to give generously and sacrificially to support it through to completion. We hoped that the bulk of the giving would be direct by church members without too much reliance on (worthy) fund-raising activities. We believed that the spiritual responses from people's hearts - touching their purses and pockets - must be paramount, and this in itself could be a powerful witness in an unbelieving and sceptical world. This was to prove abundantly true. God not only worked miracles in people's lives but also used this aspect (where money to some people is the all-important driving force) as a means of witness. Many were amazed at such generous and joyful giving.

Happily, we also had exactly the right person as our treasurer – Tina Smith! (5) Here was a person loved by everyone, full of common sense, not a professional accountant, yet able to convey money matters in a down to earth way for the lay person – not least in thinking about really big amounts beyond most people's normal experience. Her simple visual aids and sense of humour went down well. It was also significant that Tina, together with her Lay Reader husband David, were also the ones planning the special prayer days and progressive suppers - for enhancing the depth of our fellowship.

It was at this point that we made contact with various ocal and national Charitable Trusts to see if any of them might possibly be willing to give us grants. We wrote off to about a dozen and were most grateful to have gifts from 4 of them (6). We also wrote to Barings Bank, which, of course, had close historic family links within our parish and church. The Baring family lived at Mount Radford House, where Barnardo Road now stands, and they even had their own bridge built across Topsham Road to make it easier to get to church! They have a prominent family memorial under the West window in church, a large family vault outside the East entrance, and one of their family members had laid the Foundation Stone for the present church building (7). They had become one of the oldest and largest Merchant Banks in London with a world-wide reputation. Their reply to our request was brief and a little disappointing. They wrote that 'The Foundation has decided not to respond to this application for a grant. I hope you are successful in gaining the finance you seek from other sources'. We were saddened to learn that not long after this Barings Bank suffered a spectacular - and infamous - collapse. In February 1995, one of their Stock Market Traders, Nic Leeson, based in Singapore, lost £17 billion on the Japanese Futures Market, and as a direct result the great Bank folded up (8).

With hindsight, it was probably a good thing that we had to raise the bulk of the money ourselves, without relying on big donations from elsewhere. Nor did we ever have to rely on any specially big donations from within the Church Family either. The really exciting thing was that everyone contributed as much as they possibly could, and because it spanned 2 or 3 years, some donors were able to give repeat amounts in the different financial years. A great many covenanted gifts enabled us to claim tax back from the Exchequer, for this was largely before the days of Gift Aid on single gifts. Everyone rose to the challenge magnificently and generously. By God's grace everyone played their full part.

So far so good. But now what about other challenges that still lay ahead?

Chapter Seven

Unforeseen challenges

Our Architect, Alan Anderson, who had so far proved to be remarkably adaptable for the changing nature of his briefs over the previous 5-6 years, was approaching his own retirement! Little did we realise, when he was first engaged, that the whole process would take so long. But what would happen now, at such a crucial stage, in relation to the completion of the Church Centre? He had, at last, managed to achieve so much, but was now heading for Australia, for a sabbatical, which obviously meant a complete break for him and for us. The problem was whether we could find a suitable successor who would be willing to take on another person's work mid-stream, and would have had sufficient experience of this sort of specialist project? This was a crucial moment and we prayed most earnestly for God's provision and overruling to lead us to the person of his choice. He had never failed us in the past and we were confident that just the right person would be on hand.

He was! John Taylor, a highly-regarded local architect, was not only willing to help us, under these unusual circumstances, but was available. What is more, he not only had had similar experience of such a project (e.g. Truro Cathedral hall, which we were able to visit), but he also had creative flair and imagination enabling him quickly to capture our vision of what sort of Centre was needed.

One immediate example of this was that as soon as he saw Alan Anderson's drawings he realised that they were the right shape, but the wrong way round - so he swivelled them by 90 degrees. He was exactly right - as you can see today. It needed another creative mind, coming fresh to the job, to see it so clearly! (1)

He also had important new ideas in relation to interior design, appropriate materials, finishing styles, colour schemes and sliding partitions. In addition and most importantly, he also had had experience with re-constituted stone, instead of expensive original stone, and was in a strong position to convince the Planning Authorities about its suitability for our particular scheme. This alone saved us a considerable sum of money.

So much of what we see and appreciate today is due to John Taylor's flair, for even 12 years on, it still retains its fresh, pleasing appearance and has proved its durability. Many of the groups from the local authority, who started using the Centre on a regular basis often remarked that they could hardly believe they were meeting in a church hall - it was so unlike their experience of what most church halls usually look like! They were in really pleasant surroundings, without being flamboyant or expensive, and with careful maintenance and good management by our two Centre Administrators, Charles Barker and later Mike Lane, have fully retained their fresh and pristine condition. So once again God's provision and timing proved absolutely perfect. John Taylor was just the right person to take over!

Charles Barker came into the picture at this stage too, but in another unexpected role. Many church members could not make head or tail of the architect's drawings. They could not easily visualise what was proposed, and with the best will in the world, they were feeling confused. Now Charles had not only some hidden talents, but also some spare time over Christmas and the New Year. To our surprise and delight, he produced a balsa-wood 1/50th scale model of the Centre with a lift-off roof, so that all was immediately revealed inside as well as out. It was also a robust construction, strong enough to withstand constant use, by all ages to satisfy their curiosity!

The model, of course, made an immediate and dramatic visual impact (2). Suddenly, for those who found plans and drawings incomprehensible, it all became clear. Now at last they could actually see what was intended. It was one of those key moments of illumination that enabled the whole Church Family - not just the experienced specialists - to come on board the project. And it was provided free by someone who really enjoyed the challenge of producing it.

This model was to make an immediate impact on the level of pledges made at subsequent Prayer and Pledge Weekends. For many had already been pledging generously for the church refurbishment and now the Church Centre, but inevitably others had been holding back until they were clearer about the details of what was proposed. For financially, this was a considerably greater challenge than the first one (the refurbishment) as far as the total cost was concerned - and there were still a few waverers, who were not totally convinced. These were in favour of going ahead with the ground floor facilities but leaving the second floor accommodation to some later date (3). However, the vast majority were in favour of doing it all, on the grounds of needing all the accommodation at the out-set, and escalating costs if the work was delayed. There were some critical moments, with hesitations for a few, but in the end, the faith of the majority was wonderfully vindicated. For money (still in the form of pledges) kept coming in towards the daunting total of over half a million pounds. Other anonymous cash gifts (great and small) kept on arriving through the Rectory letter box - it became quite exciting to see the generosity of so many unknown donors.

Peter Elsworthy and Mike Lane (4) co-ordinated those who arranged concerts or other imaginative events towards the funds. In this way talents were offered even if money was short. Everyone wanted to play their part in some way. For God had put it into their hearts to do what they could.

We were all learning the awesome truth, spelt out in the verses from Ephesians, Chapter 3, 20-21, **'Now to Him who is able to do immeasurably more than all we ask or imagine, according to the power that is at work within us, to Him be glory in the church and in Christ Jesus, throughout all generations for ever and ever! Amen'.**

There was absolutely nothing God was unable to do. No wonder we wanted to have these inspirational verses hanging in the Entrance Hall for all to see once the Centre was built. For this was what drove us on and provided us with such encouragement. But more perseverance was still needed. We hadn't even started the building yet!

Chapter Eight

Getting planning approval for the Centre

At last our final plans for the Centre were ready, and they were submitted to the City Planners by John Taylor, who as a local architect was well known to them. They were, inevitably, examined with the utmost scrutiny, and the local Councillors held a key meeting on site. Once again they reiterated the view that this was our one and only chance to build, and, as it was such a sensitive area environmentally, we had to get it right. They, for their part, were conscious that they too were under scrutiny, having apparently had flak about one of their recent planning decisions in another part of the city. We were made aware that their standing with their electorate was at stake if they passed this scheme unwisely. The Council Planning Officers for their part were not yet happy to recommend the scheme to their Councillors without further amendments.

Their perspective was clearly much wider, too, for they started talking about the view of St. Leonard's from the other side of the canal beyond the river! The skyline of the whole city was affected, they said, especially because of the prominence of our church roof and tower. The roof had to be lowered in line with the high clerestory windows. We were therefore asked to reduce the height of the Church Centre roof and John Taylor came up with the idea of flattening it, to bring it below the skyline! (1)

The building materials also came under their close scrutiny. They were strongly in favour of original dressed stone to match that of the church, whereas John Taylor proposed re-constituted stone, specially made by a specialist firm in Somerset (2), which would be considerably cheaper, but still have a similar blend with the church. This became a sticking point until we said we would gladly comply if they gave us a grant of £30,000 to cover the extra cost - which, of course, they declined! John Taylor then produced samples, which finally convinced them that the match with the church was sufficient. The quality of the stone was high, and probably even as durable as dressed natural stone. Everyone was assured that the highest standards were being maintained and that no corners were being cut. They took a lot of convincing but clearly John Taylor's reputation for high class work counted for a great deal. They obviously held him in high regard and respected his professional judgement. Here again we had cause to thank God that he was available to help us at these key turning points. It also saved us raising a lot of extra money. (3)

Much careful thought was given to the design of the Entrance Hall which was the fulcrum for the whole integrated complex of buildings, the Centre and the Church. It was important to have as much toughened glass as possible for the frontage, so that newcomers could see clearly what was going on inside and what they were letting themselves in for, and to deter vandals. For churches generally had big oak doors which so often appeared forbidding, as if something inside was going on in secret.

We wanted everything to be as open as possible so that nothing would deter the visitor and make them feel in any way threatened. In practice, these glass doors were to give us many a headache. Wrong ones were made in Germany (4), and soon afterwards the importing firm in Bristol went out of business - but more of that anon!

One further key factor remained. Should the Church Centre be separate from the church or joined on to it? The issue only arose because of VAT! (5) If it was joined on, it would attract VAT. If it wasn't, it wouldn't! And the sum involved would have been well over £60,000, so Gordon Rice's indefatigable efforts and persistence (the VAT people seemed reluctant to put anything in writing) finally saved us a great deal of money, which in any case would do nothing to enhance the Centre.

So at last, with plans agreed, and enough money pledged to justify going out to tender, we invited sealed bids for the work, and prayed that God would overrule the outcome. Six large firms submitted tenders (6), and it was quite an exciting moment when all the bids were opened. There was a considerable variation between them, but the lowest was from a large and reputable Plymouth firm, Dudley Coles Ltd, who we gathered were anxious to obtain a foothold in the Exeter area, and were looking for just such a prestigious project to establish themselves here. In due course, once the building was under way, their Managing Director spoke at a meeting to tell us about their work.

The Contract was signed on June 7th 1993. This was greeted with huge relief by church members, who after a long 2½ years of waiting since the refurbishment of the church had been completed, were now embarking on the building of this much needed accommodation! For at least 7 years such expansion had been envisaged - well before the fire came to our rescue in such dramatic fashion - and now the contract for the work had actually been signed, and things were starting to take shape.   In the Letter of James (7) it says that 'the testing of your faith develops perseverance. Perseverance must finish its work, so that you may be mature and complete not lacking anything'. It says also that this is linked closely with wisdom from God to begin to understand what He is doing through the tests. Yes, God was unmistakably at work through all these processes.

Chapter Nine

Building begins at last

The contractors, Dudley Coles, with Keith Bygraves as their Works Manager, moved in on Monday, August 16th, 1993. First their portakabins were installed in the main car parking area and the whole of the working site was surrounded by a high security fence. Access to the church reverted to the narrow front door, and all the approaches to the church grounds had to be kept open for constant use, but everyone coped with the inevitable disruption admirably and there were no accidents.

For the contractors the access to the site for the Centre was extremely narrow, and everything either had to pass in front of the Vestry door or be lifted bodily over the surrounding trees, which all had a protection order on them. Great care had to be taken that nothing was damaged.

There was some exceptionally skilful manoeuvring by the JCB digger operators and the heavy concrete-mixer lorry drivers - and of course the operators of the huge cranes, lifting heavy machinery over the top. It made one wonder how previous generations managed with the narrow access roads and the high walls all around. Four church buildings of different sizes have occupied the site since the 12th Century. For them, foundations were also an important factor, for the previous building before the present one, described as an 'handsome Grecian edifice' had to be pulled down because of collapsing walls. Then the present tower was apparently so heavy that it had to have concrete foundations down below the level of Larkbeare Road, by the present Judge's Lodgings. Some depth!

The foundations for the Centre were being laid in uncharted territory for the most part. That part of the graveyard had been unused for well over 100 years. However, any disturbance was kept to the absolute minimum by the Contractors, and they showed great skill and sensitivity. (1)

We are grateful to many others who showed great patience at the time. These were our close neighbours in St. Leonard's Avenue and Weirfield Road. They not only put up with great parking inconvenience but also with other disruptions and extra noise. We made special efforts to warn them well in advance of what was likely to happen, and when the Centre was eventually opened they were given early escorted tours. We had much restraint and understanding from them at the time and valued their forbearance.

After the deep foundation work was completed, the huge framework girders had to be set in place, as well as the pre-cast concrete blocks for the upper floor and the staircases. These, of course, had to be lifted into place high over the line of trees and made spectacular viewing. One of the largest mobile cranes was set up in St. Leonard's Avenue to await the lorries arriving from the North of England, at set intervals, together with an army of experts to install them at remarkable speed. Now the Centre was really beginning to take shape.

The next huge job was the arrival and special storage of a vast quantity of re-constituted stone, all in specially numbered consignments. This was a particularly complex operation, because each individual stone was specially 'mottled', and all had to be numbered and set in place separately. The bricklayers were given special charts to work to, in order to get the effect exactly right, to blend in with the church stonework. This also took time and patience - and not a little skill. One of the bricklayers was particularly interested in the work - he was a churchwarden at a church in Torquay!

Then a team of carpenters moved in to begin work on the roof, the heavy beams again being lifted in over the top of the trees. Meanwhile large quantities of Welsh slate (2) were arriving which would give such a superb finish to the building and blend in so well with the church surroundings. Already it was becoming clear that all the careful planning and design - and amendments - had been justified, for even when viewed from the other side of the river, it was all exactly right!

When the time came for digging deep trenches through the approaches to the church, for linking on to the main drainage mains, there was inevitably considerable disruption, not just for those coming to church on foot, but also for traffic in Topsham Road. At least all the passers-by knew by now that something really major was taking place at St. Leonard's - of that there could be no doubt.

Now that the Centre had been enclosed externally, work could begin on the interior with wiring teams, plumbing teams and finally plastering teams all playing their part. After the drying-out process, the carpenters moved in, and now we were beginning to see some of the special wood that John Taylor had selected, which would give such a pleasing effect to the whole design, not least throughout the large hall, with its huge, sound-proof partitions. No wonder subsequent users were to express their admiration for such congenial surroundings in which to meet.

The final part to be completed was the all-important Entrance Hall and the two connections between the Centre and the Church. Glass panelled doors (3) replaced the solid oak ones leading into the church - again provided to give the sense of openness - and the temporary kitchenette in the tower was removed to gain a second route through. First impressions were so important as the Entrance Hall served as our welcome area. It was also important for groups using the Centre to be able to look into the church itself through a glass door. They could then see clearly that the building was an integrated whole.

As the work neared completion, we were given permission to have some conducted tours for members of the congregation, so eager to see for themselves what the (nearly) finished Centre was like. News spread rapidly about how magnificent it was - and well worth waiting for. Already there was great rejoicing, not least that the Centre would open completely free of debt. All the money - well over half a million pounds - had been gladly given! Praise God!

Chapter Ten

The
Centre ready to open

Exactly on schedule the Church Centre was completed (1) (apart from those troublesome glass doors) on July 1st 1994, nearly 5 years after the fire. There was a great sense of anticipation and excitement, as the congregation entered the church, via the Centre for the first time.

There was a temporary Welcome Desk, replaced later by a professionally crafted one by Robin Furlong and presented by the whole family. Then to the left of the church entrance hung a full-length tapestry made by a gifted team led by Anita Beasley, with well over 600 names lovingly woven into it of most of the members of the Church Family at the time. To the right hung the framed verses from Ephesians 3 : 20-21 which had inspired us all so greatly throughout the refurbishing and the rebuilding. Both these visual aids were to be a constant reminder in the coming years of how faithful and generous God had been to us. It was something which had been written indelibly on our lives too.

It was immediately apparent to all how superbly the two buildings (the Church and Centre) had been unified. They both merged amazingly into one as you went from one into the other and the whole complex was equally to the Glory of God throughout - worship and fellowship were inextricably intertwined and integrated as they should be.

Two weeks later we had the first of our two celebration weekends. Following our established custom, the whole of Saturday was devoted to praise and prayer, and a great number throughout the day gathered to express their gratitude to God. That same evening, Tina Smith organised another of her Progressive Suppers, when people visited numerous homes for different courses, mixing everyone up along the way, before all uniting at the end at the Centre for coffee and more fellowship! The Centre was crowded and people seemed in no hurry to leave!

At the special Thanksgiving Services next day, we had two former Curates as our preachers - Roy Henderson, (2) Vicar of St. Mary's, Stoke Bishop in Bristol and Curate here from 1954-57, in the morning, and Alastair Wallace, Rector of St. Michael's and St. Paul's, Bath and Curate here from 1975–79, in the evening.

Two weeks later the Holiday Club, with about 200 children, met for the first time in the Centre and Church, having of course, previously been in the Church Hall in Roberts Road. The whole building was alive with purposeful activity and the upstairs rooms were particularly popular.

The official Dedication Sunday was then held on Sunday, September 25th 1994, when invitations were sent to all those who had been involved in the construction of the Centre including, of course, all the workmen and their families. The church was packed for both Services, with closed-circuit television for those in an overflow area – such was the congestion. The Bishop of Exeter, Hewlett Thompson, spoke from 1 Corinthians 3 at the morning service, totally engulfed by children sitting on the carpet all around him, with not a space to spare, before leading

View of the brighter interior and vastly improved lighting

The carpeting throughout added colour and warmth

*A clear view of the Baring family memorial, alongside the
original rear entrance, now an alternative way to the centre*

Some of the relocated choir stalls

Nearly 400 comfortable chairs arrive

II(C)

(Below) The connecting door from the church to the Centre unifying the whole complex

Paul Dawson and Penny Gray (with Geoff Hobden, a former curate on the right) after their wedding on 22 April 1990, outside the narrow church entrance on the north side which, had to be used for four years, until the centre was built, causing considerable congestion and inconvenience. But somehow we managed!

All the furniture in place

III(C)

The flexibility of the layout was an enormous advantage

This was a layout for a harvest assembly for the Central Middle School, who sat on the carpet, with parents on chairs at the back

The Chancel area, with a moveable Communion Rail was adaptable for Sunday and weekday use, and for drama and concerts

IV(C)

The first service in the refurbished Church

A good view for the dozens of children crammed into the Chancel

The Holiday Club used every part of the Church (and eventually the Centre). It was so colourful and welcoming

V(C)

Looking at other church extensions (here a view of St. Matthias, Torquay, where we gleaned many ideas from a Church Away-Day) gave us inspiration for our future plans

David and Tina Smith arranged all the Prayer and Pledge Weekends. Tina was Church Treasurer and David a Lay Reader, an excellent team! John Hill (right) a Church Member, and Architect

Charles and Joyce Hocking. Charles was a Churchwarden in the '70's. Joyce was a successful Girl Covenanter Leader for many years and led the Women's Fellowship

VI(C)

Above: Steve, Anna and Joshua Griffiths, now with OMF in Singapore (with daughter Aimee)
Right: Tom and Hazel Davis. Tom was an architect and Hazel helped with the Children's work
Below: David and Mary Banks. David was Gordon Rice's fellow Church Warden at the time of the fire

Top: David and Heather Sharland (with CMS in Africa) with Marilyn Skinner.
Left: Rosie Hutchinson before she met Dan Button! Now with Crosslinks in Uganda
Bottom: Chris and Alison Hawksbee with SAMS in Paraguay South America-Just three of our missionary couples

them and the rest of the congregation (rather like a Pied-Piper) down the aisle into the Centre (on a circular route) ending up in the main hall for a brief ceremony and a magnificent buffet lunch (3). He was quite moved by the whole experience, and so were we! And our special guests entered fully into the spirit of the whole joyous occasion, which proved an unforgettable witness to the love, provision and goodness of God. The evening Thanksgiving Service was no less memorable as the church was again crowded to hear the Archdeacon of Exeter, Tony Tremlett, who together with his wife Pat, had been members of St. Leonard's before he entered the ministry. He spoke from Psalm 103 about God's never-failing goodness. Most people stayed on long after the service and again seemed reluctant to leave.

So much interest had been aroused locally that many open evenings ('At homes') were arranged by members living in different sections of the parish, personally inviting all their neighbours and friends to join them - and they then acted as hosts for that particular evening in the Centre. Most of the parish was covered in this way, and many new local friendships were formed. In fact several hundred visitors must have been welcomed in this way during these week-days and for Sunday services, not least Harvest Thanksgiving and subsequent Guest Services and Family Services.

Our great vision was now entering a completely new era and was being wonderfully fulfilled. At last we were really on the move - praise God!

Chapter Eleven

The outworking of the vision - what now?

It was hard to believe, at first, that after so many years of privation and severe restriction, we now had the full use of these superb new premises for God's work : It was almost too good to be true!   So after the inevitable (and justifiable) euphoria had died down just a little, we set about ensuring that everything would be profitably used for the furtherance of the Gospel.   God had graciously provided us with such magnificent facilities, not only for our own comfort or benefit, but even more to reach out further to those who needed to know more about the love of God in Christ.   For that had been our over-riding objective all along, with the special (though by no means exclusively) focus on families.   God had been faithful to us. We must ensure that we remained faithful to Him.

It needs to be remembered that most other churches were, at this time, struggling both to reach children and families, or to cope with the few they had.   The gap between the old and the young was getting even greater, and with the best will in the world, once this trend had begun, it was incredibly difficult to reverse.   This in fact was the current state of affairs in many churches of all denominations.   How fortunate we were, therefore, not only to have such a superb team to lead over 250 or so young people, but now tailor-made premises for them to meet in as well!

Many spiritually concerned parents were only too glad to find such lively children's activities, which their children would look forward to and actually enjoy!. Sundays were not boring. They were not dragged reluctantly to church. No! They actually looked forward to Sundays! To see the amazement on new parents' faces, as they walked hand in hand with their children approaching the church, to find the child suddenly releasing hands to run on ahead! They could hardly get there quickly enough. It was a heart-warming sight to witness! So now the parents themselves could relax, knowing their children were so happy and well looked after in their groups - and as near at hand too.

The large Crèche room, named after Mary Brice (1), was now crawling with babies and toddlers, and having the modern nappy changing room on hand was a great boon. (2) The sound-proof partitions subdivided the rest of the hall for two other groups of smaller children, and there were two additional groups upstairs (with toilets and a superb kitchenette as well as plenty of storage space). There was a great atmosphere throughout the integrated premises, as, from 0 - 90, the whole church family not only heard more about the love and grace of God, but also felt it as well! It had truly developed into a deeply loving church family - which so many people commented upon. The Lord's presence was powerfully at work among his people, young and old alike. Jesus, after all, had said to his disciples, 'Love one another. As I have loved you so you must love one another. All men will know that you are my disciples if you love one another'. (John 13 v.34). So here it was in practice. Careful thought had been given to the running of the Centre and Charles Barker was appointed as Administrator. We were so fortunate that someone of his vision and experience was now available to help in this key capacity since he had just retired early from the world of business and accountancy. We also knew that he had great enthusiasm for the job, having so painstakingly built the scale model for us, which was such a turning point for the church members at a critical stage. He immediately proved to be the ideal person, and apart from his efficiency and enterprise, took great delight in personally showing visitors, individuals and groups around. Nothing was too much trouble and no-one too much bother, however busy he was. Working from the Church Office in the Vestry, he dovetailed so smoothly with the existing office team under Margaret Unsworth's capable and patient leadership. They had been working under such duress while all the work had been in progress. How we thanked God for such a dedicated team serving the Lord in this practical way! (3)

Obviously church groups had priority use of the Centre, and about 25 groups used the premises on a regular basis. Other local Christian organisations, including Diocesan groups, (their Councils, Training Courses and Lunches and the Diocesan Evangelical Fellowship), ICE(4), working in local schools, Crossline, a counselling ministry, Christian Response to Eastern Europe - and various others. Then national groups like Scripture Union and the Church Pastoral Aid Society, the Bible Society and many others used the premises for their regular area meetings.

We were also greatly encouraged that several non-church groups wanted to come. Devon County Council, for example, used it for their Social Services, Education,

Personnel and Environment groups; Devon Services used it for their Probation, Library, Age Concern, National Childbirth Trust, Child Minding groups. The International Tree Foundation enjoyed using it also. In reporting to the Church Charles Barker could write that 'this secular group increase has occurred through word of mouth recommendations. We have not approached any outside organisation to seek bookings from them, in fact we have declined many bookings we could have taken, so that accommodation would be available for church use if required'. The surroundings were pleasant, the parking was available, the locality was convenient, and we were able to subdivide the premises easily (with an upstairs kitchenette) so that two or three groups could use the facilities simultaneously. (5) It is also worth adding that the Centre was much in demand for receptions after funerals, baptisms and weddings - not least as a preliminary reception centre for church members, before going on to their formal hotel reception. Additionally, and most importantly, it was greatly used for much personal counselling by Maggie Barker and her team.

The Centre was virtually self-financing from the donations (rather than fees) of outside groups using it. Far from it being a burden to church funds, it sometimes had a surplus for general funds. Fortunately we had a wonderful group of cleaners and caterers, who saw their work as part of their Christian Service - and how well they did it! (6)

Questions were constantly raised about the future role of the hall in Roberts Road. Would it still be needed? Should it be sold to help pay for the Centre? What about our local witness in that part of the parish?

How would it suffer if the hall was under used or neglected? Clearly a well-maintained hall in Roberts Road would still be needed for the foreseeable future, so the PCC drew up a plan for its refurbishment and maintenance. (7)

One key church group that had to be constantly re-located was Centre-Point for Prayer. It had an enforced nomadic life, rather like Abraham! Burnt out of house and home in the old Foyer, it transferred to Roberts Road. When the Church was refurbished it moved to the Church Chancel, and eventually when the Centre was up and running it found its settled base there.   Our surroundings were secondary to the truth that God met wherever his people met in the name of Jesus, and our greatest privilege was to 'carry everything to God in prayer', knowing that our reliance, especially under pressure, must always be on him.   For Jesus said to his disciples, 'Without me you can do nothing', and 'with me all things are possible' (8) . How true!

Chapter Twelve

And finally -
the bigger picture

As we conclude this remarkable story, we now need to ask the key question; What do we believe God was seeking to do behind the scenes throughout this whole episode? If we stand back, is it possible to discern how it all fits together? How did St. Leonard's, both people and premises, need to be changed, urgently and radically, as the challenges of the new Millennium were drawing near? What was happening in the rapidly changing world around, culturally and spiritually, when the majority of people would be unchurched and dominated by secular attitudes? What would be needed to ensure that St. Leonard's was not to be hopelessly left behind and regarded as an archaic irrelevance? To put it starkly: 'What would have happened if there had been no fire - and no change? Would St. Leonard's have been stuck in a time-warp, ill-equipped for relevant and fruitful witness in the 21st Century?

But just how sure can we be about God's attitudes and aims? Might we be presumptuous in trying to second-guess what He was doing? This is certainly a possible danger. But Scripture spells out his longings very clearly. We read, for instance, that **'God our Saviour wants all men to be saved and to come to the knowledge of the truth. For there is one God and one mediator between God and man, Christ Jesus who gave himself as a ransom for all men'**. (1) It could hardly be stated more clearly than that, and Jesus sent Christians out with a personal mandate to proclaim this saving Gospel to all. This is, therefore, the enormous privilege for all Christians in Exeter, including ourselves!

Now, as has become clearly apparent already, faith-sharing has long had a prominent emphasis at St. Leonard's, shown not least by strong support for overseas missions. Over many years and during many faithful ministries, this has been enhanced by a team of ardent missionary reps (2), regular missionary prayer groups, personal reports from home-coming missionaries, not to mention the many inspiring visiting missionary speakers!

However, granted all this, had an imbalance between overseas and home faith-sharing inadvertently crept in? Was the deep awareness and concern for witness on distant shores clouding the huge needs and changes on our own doorstep? Quite possibly, though it has to be said that these same missionary reps (along with many others of like mind) clearly showed the full scope of their vision when major decisions over re-building were taking place. Their strong public lead at these critical moments was vital and decisive. For their part, there was no doubt at all about what should be done!

So if that is the bigger picture, what was God wanting to do specifically in and through St. Leonard's during those 10 eventful years? What was His programme, and how was He going to use adversity to promote his good purposes?

First: God, it seems, was seeking to re-establish both a vibrant mission community and provide us with a modern mission base for effective and fruitful witness in the new era ahead, not least among families.

Second: God, it seems, wanted to achieve both these objectives simultaneously (and inter-actively) within the same time scale, so that both could be fully operational together.

Third: God, it seems, was using the five preliminary years before the fire as a trial run for all that was to follow. He was re-testing our mettle in relation to our vision, perseverance, unity, prayerfulness and patience. Only after that would we then clear the ground ahead, dramatically and literally! (3)

So now perhaps, we can spell out in more detail some of the major spiritual developments during those years, focused more sharply, and possibly hastened, by the unfolding circumstances.

First, and foremost, was an enhanced grasp of the greatness of God! As our Almighty Father, absolutely nothing was impossible for him. He alone could open doors that had previously been firmly locked and bolted! It was not only awesome to watch as spectators but He was also at work inside us as well. We were on His workshop bench as He moulded and re-conditioned us. It was a tremendous privilege to be caught up in what He was doing so evidently. The living God was seen to be visibly at work!

Second, this was, of course, most clearly reflected in our corporate attitudes in prayer, when the regular church prayer meeting was re-named Centre-Point for Prayer to bring this truth home. Prayer was central for everything and **everyone.** 'For our Sovereign God was able to do immeasurably <u>more</u> than all we ask or imagine, according to His power that is at work within us.' (4) This was so obviously the case, that these two verses were framed and hung in the Church Entrance as a testimony of our experience for all to see. We wanted to shout it from the rooftops - it's true! Whether it was prayer together on Sundays, special days of prayer, praying in groups, prayer triplets, prayer at the PCC and Building Group - it permeated all our Church prayer life in a new and deepened way. Far from being stuck in one-eyed prayers, only for our own immediate circumstances, we embraced the full gamut of worldwide need, not least for evangelistic outreach, our own included! Our priority of mission never wavered and it was encouraging to see so many of all ages coming to a personal faith in Christ throughout these upheavals.

<u>Third</u>, it proved to be a considerable faith-stretching process, especially in relation to giving. Large sums of money were being asked for, well beyond the experience of many up to that point, and at times, a few understandably expressed their doubts as to whether this was both right and possible. One particular hurdle - for some - came during a critical church meeting when key decisions were being taken about the Church Centre. The issue was : 'Would we have enough money to build the <u>whole</u> Church Centre, or should we settle for the ground-floor only, and postpone the upper storey until some time later?' What would the choice be? At that point, one of our highly respected and most missionary-minded members, Tom Davis, spoke up, 'We must do it <u>all</u> now', he said, 'and we firmly believe that such a generous God will provide all the necessary resources!' The vast majority agreed - and, of course, God did provide!

The underlying test all along was whether, in relation to generous Christian giving, we had all really understood the truth of Jesus' statement. 'It is more blessed to give than to receive' (5) . Had we truly experienced how wonderfully liberating this could be? It was, in fact, a slow learning curve, rather than a sudden conclusion, as first smaller hurdles, then bigger hurdles were placed in front of us, spanning a period of time - until the huge final total was achieved and all was completely paid for - or so we thought!

But there was one more final test to come, which could so easily have proved one test too far. In all our joy and relief, we suddenly discovered that one final bill - for £30,000! - had been unknowingly incurred! What would be the reaction of the Church on the Sunday, when the PCC disclosed the true picture? Dismay? Incredulity? Blame? No way! The response was immediate. All the extra money was given by the very next Sunday by the whole congregation - not just through the generosity of a few. The collective joy was unbounded! They had proved what Jesus had said. It was more blessed to give than to receive! A totally new attitude towards giving had been established at St. Leonard's and there was to be no going back. God's grace was powerfully and practically at work in people's hearts, for that is where true giving begins.

Fourth, and most significantly for the future proclamation of the Gospel, St. Leonard's grew into a much more oving Christian Community. Visitors began to comment on it. It was something that they both saw and felt, and was so noticeably in contrast to the world outside! This was to prove an increasingly powerful dimension of witness, because it was a living dimension of the Gospel. It was reflecting, of course, what Jesus himself had said to his disciples, 'As I have loved you, so you must love one another. <u>By this</u> will all men know that you are my disciples if you show love one to another' (6) . Clearly an unloving church is not only a denial of the Gospel, but it is a most unattractive witness! Someone has rightly said, 'People are often attracted to a Christian Community before they are attracted to the Christian message....the challenge is to ensure that people see our love for one another. We need to introduce people to the network of believing relationships'.(7) If this unique divine love, "poured into our hearts by the Holy Spirit"(8), is sustained, in every mission community of Christian people, it will surely be a vital factor in our increasingly pluralistic society. Pray to God that it will attract many more to experience personally the saving love of God in Christ for themselves as a direct result!

So finally - what a fantastic head start for vibrant witness God has seen fit to give St. Leonard's! - and all through that fire and that one match! It has been well said that **'the church exists for mission as a fire exists for burning'**.(9) For St. Leonard's that was literally true as both fire and mission have been so closely allied and intertwined throughout this story! No wonder, therefore, we can say with heartfelt conviction 'Thank God, indeed, for that fire!' But now we can also say, 'Thank God for the enormous new mission opportunities that have opened up as a result of the fire', which we must continue to take to the full. For God himself prepared both His people (10) and their premises for all that He knew lay ahead for them in the 21st Century - who struck the match? - we do not know - but God lit the fire!

Appendix

The fire - from the Treasurer's perspective

by Tina Smith

I had just taken over as Treasurer when the fire occurred. I came back from a week away in London to discover that the fire had happened and that an army of people including the insurers had moved in on the church building. Gordon Rice had known who to contact and I was given a cheque for £10,000 from the insurers to pay for the initial clean up and to enable us to have a breathing space while we sorted out what to do next.

The priority was the church services on the Sunday and a very special wedding of a deaf couple the following Saturday. The cleaners moved in. The Foyer was declared unusable and the entrances screened by plants and all attention focused on the church. Bibles were stripped of their protective plastic and were found to be usable. Hymn books were cleaned. Chairs were washed down and the seating pads thrown out as too smoke logged to be any use. The walls and pillars were scrubbed to about ten foot from floor level. By Friday evening the church was clean enough to use and the services could be held in the church. The organ at that point was usable.

The Sunday saw us all rejoicing in God's hand in conjunction with the Fire Brigade, an alert neighbour and the member of the clergy who managed to get to the church with a key to allow access to the building before everything had gone up in smoke.

We then sat back and had time to reflect and count the cost, to decide what needed to be done and the order of priority. The plans for an extension to the Foyer were then put on the back burner while the damage was assessed. The Buildings Committee and the PCC had had their minds focused. The treasurer's job had changed overnight. No longer were we raising money for a project in some indeterminate future; we had to act now. Although there was some discussion about having a separate Treasurer for the appeal, I was willing to do the job - it had been hard enough to find a Church Treasurer! I don't think that I - or anyone else - really realised how big the job would be.

The money from insurance would allow us to redecorate and restore what had been damaged as it had been but the vision was bigger. This was an opportunity to redesign the church to give more flexibility and to look closely at what we wanted in the way of other rooms and facilities.

Once again the decision was made to focus our attention on the church. With an architect plans were drawn up to refurbish the church. An initial budget of £70,000 for this work was drawn up and we considered how we could raise the money. This was as much as the previous year's total budget for the church. The Finance Committee and the PCC felt that as "the cattle on a thousand hills" belonged to God we should be seen to trust God at all stages in raising this money. We felt that most of the money should come from the committed, sacrificial giving by the members of the congregation. We also felt that we should not make a public appeal as we felt that God's work should be supported by God's people.

Under taxation and charitable laws existing at the time, people could make covenanted payments to charities, so long as the covenant lasted for at least four years, and was for the same regular sum. But the only way that one could give a lump sum to a charity and recover tax was to use a "deposit covenant", making the gift as a loan. Part of this loan would become each year's charitable donation. This complicated scheme for transforming gifts into covenanted gifts meant a great deal of paperwork, and because of the difficulties in administering it, often went wrong and so was not popular.

But this was the year when the Chancellor of the Exchequer announced in his spring Budget statement that there would be a new tax concession on single gifts of over £600. Gifts of this size would be tax recoverable, and the paperwork was simpler. As Treasurer I wondered if this new Gift Aid (as it was called) would make any difference as £600 seemed a very large gift for one person to make.

The church had a gift day and asked people to consider whether they could give in such a way that the Chancellor (or, more accurately, the Government) would contribute too. For tax payers giving by covenant over a period of four or more years made the gifts tax recoverable. However the Gift Aid rules would only come into effect in six months time. Neither way of giving was going to be in time for the immediate need. So we asked people to loan the church the money. If they could give over £600, we would then return the loan when Gift Aid was allowed, and then they could give the money as Gift Aid. For people, who could make a lump sum gift smaller than £600, we asked them to make it as a loan to be converted into four equal gifts payable under covenant. Hopefully, if several people made deposit covenants, we would be able to handle them efficiently and without the usual difficulties.

Enough money was pledged to allow the work on the church interior to start. As the bills came in, so month by month did the money. Worshipping in the Royal School for the Deaf stretched our resources in other directions. People who could not pledge money made offers of time and manpower and these were taken up. We were working together.

As we moved back into the church there were still costs that came in that had not been anticipated. God was faithful. We saw each bill met on time with money to spare in the bank. As Treasurer I had to announce that we had gone over budget, and that it was difficult to know the final figure. We spent more than £100,000 on the church interior.

Then an unexpected request arrived from the Inland Revenue; they wished to inspect the church's account books. I knew that this was possible in theory, and that some churches had had claims for covenants disallowed, if the paper trail (the documentation that recorded each stage of a gift, from donor, through the bank, to tax claim) was not accurate. Over the previous few years we had tried to get all covenants paid through the bank to establish a clear trail. Those paid through the envelope scheme in cash had to be recorded very carefully. I arranged to meet the inspector and prepared for the meeting with all our record books.

When the man arrived he said that we were among the highest reclaimers of tax in the U.K. under the new Gift Aid rules. (I had known that we were unusual, because I had telephoned the Gift Aid office several times for more of their forms, and by the third or fourth time, I was known to them as "The lady who uses lots of forms".) He examined each gift checking the dates on the forms and the dates the money was paid into the bank. When he realised that much of the money had been on loan for the previous six months, he checked that the loans had been physically repaid rather than just transferred from loans to gifts in the record books. I was very grateful to the people, who had checked and established the procedures to meet the very strict criteria for tax to be reclaimed. He was surprised and almost seemed disappointed that the tax claim was valid! He then went through the same procedure on the covenants. He actually found an error, a deposit covenant had been made into a gift on the wrong date and we so we could not reclaim the tax on it. As a result, we had claimed £1.26 too much. He then went through the envelope scheme. I was glad that not many people gave weekly envelopes (because every envelope had to be counted and recorded) and that the paper trail was all there (even if it did fill a carrier bag each year). Five hours later he agreed that the procedures were correct and we were entitled to the tax we had claimed.

God's timing had been perfect. Gift Aid had encouraged people to think large in terms of giving and we had all learnt valuable lessons. God could even get the Chancellor to contribute to rebuilding His house.

The harder part was still to come, but we had begun. The church was refurbished although the organ was no longer working properly. The corrosive effects of soot on delicate electrical items were making themselves   felt. However, the organ was not a priority. We now needed to tackle the burnt out shell of the Foyer.

The architect and the building committee were in negotiations with the city council about what would be possible on the site. The finance group was in negotiation with the insurers and an appeal went out for photographs of the Church Foyer before the fire. Could we prove that the cracking of the ring beam happened as a result of the fire? Suddenly everything seemed to come together. The cracked beam meant we had to pull the Foyer down. The photographs of parties and meetings in the Foyer showed no signs of the damage before the fire and a figure was agreed with the insurance company. A new architect and a clear site meant a different approach and agreement in principle with the council and various other interested parties. The architect presented outline plans to the church. Our response was "WOW!" The plans had an excitement of their own and we felt we were up and flying.

The plans went to costing and money was trickling in. There was no major gift other than the insurance money. As a church we were still feeling the effects of the giving for the interior of the church.

The Finance Committee met to consider the cost estimates from the architect. I had felt concerned and had been driven to pray before the meeting. Tom Davis, whom I met on my way home from work, knew about the meeting and promised to pray for our discussions. His attitude heartened me as he reminded me that "God's work, done in God's way, does not lack God's resources" (or words to that effect). While the meeting still did not know the precise figures we were asked to consider how much we felt the church could be asked to give.

The committee was getting depressed and bogged down when we decided to look at it from the other end. How much would the building cost? The estimated cost of the construction work was £300,000. We expected that we would need a little bit more to make everything really attractive. Some members of the committee felt that it was out of the question to try to raise such a huge amount. During prayer we decided to ask God for a sign. If we should go ahead, there should be at least a tenth of that money already in the bank.

I pulled out the books and my calculator. Normally I only added columns up at the bottom of a page so, not having computerised accounts, I had no total figures ready. I added the column up once and again before I believed my eyes and dared announce it to the group. We already had more than £60,000, a fifth of the estimate, and more than twice what we had asked God for. He wanted us to go forward and was giving His seal of approval on the project.

So we needed to raise, roughly, a quarter of a million pounds. This still seemed a huge mountain to climb. How could we break down the figure into sums that church members could understand? We tried dividing the sum by the number of people on the church family list and working out how many Mars bar equivalents each man, woman and child would have to give every week for four years. (250 people - about £5 each a week - about 20 Mars bars each). This was a slightly ridiculous illustration as we didn't know anyone, who would go out and buy 20 Mars bars in a week. We knew that most people could not hope to give £5 a week, particularly not the children. We then wondered what if some people could give £5,000 and others £50 in a year. How many gifts of that size would we need to climb the money mountain?

The next gift weekend came with a leaflet illustrating various ways of giving. People were reminded that, although we would have to pay VAT on the building, the Chancellor was willing to contribute towards the building, if we paid tax and were prepared to commit our giving by covenant or Gift Aid. The Saturday was given over to prayer. On the Sunday we accepted pledges.

People responded in whatever way they could. One child pledged his weekly sweets (and the first week it came in as sweets - which his dad redeemed). Some offered their time. Others offered support in various ways.

The Finance Committee decided to try to count the pledges during the day so that we could announce the totals at the end of each service whilst keeping confidentiality. So the treasurer and Covenant secretary were busy. By the final hymn of each service a total had been reached.

It was far more than I had expected. We had enough to start the building expecting that, with hard work, we could raise more money. However we had not reached the total amount needed to complete the project. I went home that Sunday exhausted and elated.

A phone call came in from one parent. Please could I explain to their son how I could say that God was answering our prayers when the full quarter of a million pounds had not been pledged? It took a little while to explain to a lad of about ten that God had inspired His people to give enough actual cash for the building to start, and promises of other sorts to keep us trusting that He would provide the rest of the money in His time and in His ways.

Looking back over the whole project I can say it was a faith stretching time. Bills came in and always there was enough money in the bank to be able to write the cheque to meet them without delay. I did not want to keep people waiting for payment because I felt that would dishonour God who was in overall control. God was in control of the money!

Finance for the project came in all sorts of ways.

First there was the sacrificial giving of God's people. I do not know how many people gave up their home extensions to see the extension to God's house finished first, or the people, who did not go on holiday. There were those, who gave up a lifetime's dream because God came first, and those, who week by week set aside a little extra, which meant they had less for luxuries and essentials themselves.

Then there were those who gave freely and generously of their time. Committees who considered fund raising, people who cleaned, babysat and ran errands. Little by little, and occasionally a lot by a lot, the money came in-and so did the realisation that the building was going to need to be decorated, furnished, equipped and maintained. The God who could control the money for the building could control that too.

There were a few special events, which united the church for a celebration and the joy of doing something together.

God, who was at work teaching us that He was in control of money, was also in control of uniting the church family. We had a project to work at - and the memorial quilt in the centre lists the names of those, who wished to be associated with it. We worked hard together and had a lot of fun. Fund raising took many different forms: concerts, plant sales, mugs, cards, cook books. Some of these did not raise much money but they raised awareness and built friendships, giving time to work and play together.

Meanwhile the cost of the project rose above the estimate of £300,000 - the original challenge had been to raise a quarter of a million pounds, and many had doubted that we could do that. Gradually, there were other costs of the project. We decided to do the best we could "while we were at it", so there were extra costs of construction, furnishings, and professional charges. Eventually, the church raised almost half a million pounds for the centre, five times the "huge" sum that had been needed for refurbishing the church itself.

The major work was completed and there was a PCC meeting at which the architect was going to be present as we discussed the completion of the project. As Treasurer I was grateful the work was complete and we were able to hold the meeting in one of the upstairs rooms of the centre. We could use the building. As I walked out of my house to attend the meeting, I suddenly turned around and picked up the books, not that I felt I needed them, but because they were a testament to God's faithfulness over the project. By this time I was using a spreadsheet on the computer to keep running totals, so a quick print out allowed me to see the amounts that had come in over the whole project as well as the current balance.

The architect told us that he had an apology to make to the PCC. We were all surprised. He then said that the final bill would be a lot larger than anticipated. Not only were his professional fees in it, but it also included the extras and the changes that had happened as the project had developed. How was the PCC to react? I dug for the books and quickly turned to the relevant page. I said "The money to meet this increased bill is already in the bank. We might not have known of it but God did." The prayer session that followed was a time of praise and thanksgiving. God had been seen to be in control.

We needed to look at the amount of that final bill because, although enough money was in the bank, we had been expecting to use it for the final furnishings and fittings. As a PCC, we decided to go to the church and explain about this extra bill. The response was swift and the generosity of people amazing. There were further bills to come in, some for things that we didn't realise we would need, like blinds for the windows, but bill by bill the money had always been there.

Footnotes

Introduction

(1)   One of these was Larkbeare House, owned by John Baring, who had a local cloth business. His Elizabethan House stood where Roberts Road now joins Topsham Road and was demolished in 1889. Another large house, Mount Radford, was built by John Baring in 1775, became a school in 1827 and was demolished in 1902, when Barnardo Road and Cedars Road were built. It had most of the present St. Leonard's Road as its grand drive way. Other large local homes were Coaver and Bellair now part of County Hall.

(2)   The new young Rector was J. F. Sheldon, appointed in 1887. It was just 2 years later that the foundation stone for the Roberts Road hall was laid. He stayed at St. Leonard's until 1896, when he moved to lead a church at Cromer in Norfolk. He later returned to St. Leonard's from 1912-1922.   His great grandson, Chris Sheldon, is a current member of St. Leonard's - continuing the close and active family association.

(3)   You will see from the photograph on page V(A) that the foundation stone of the hall was in memory of George William Petter, who was also the great grandfather of Dr. Nora Sims. With her husband Dr. Charles she was in medical practice in Southernhay with Dr. Keith Lockhart, an outstanding stalwart at St. Leonard's over many, many years.   The Sims were leaders in Belmont Chapel, and the links between the two churches have always been close.

(4)   Quoted from an article, about church improvements, in the Church of England Newspaper, by kind permission.

Clearing the ground

*Building firm foundations. Clearly the new Church
door on the left could not be used!*

*The Judges Lodging's (for the Assize Court) are visible
through the framework*

I(D)

Fund raising was greatly helped by Charles Barker's balsa wood model. Now people could grasp what the centre would be like. Unfortunately we have no picture of the model, only this amusing cartoon of it!

So charles, how much balsa wood will you need for the real "thing?

II(D)

Above: Concrete blocks, brought down from the North Midlands had to be lifted high over the Holm Oaks.
Right: There was no other way in.
Below: View from the new first floor, looking back towards the car park .

View from the other side of the river Exe. The City Council said that the roof must be flattened, not to spoil the profile of St. Leonard's from a distance

Extensive view from the first floor roof towards Haldon Hill

The tiles were of Welsh slate, matching those of the Church

Above: The upstairs corridor, taken from the new kitchenette

Right: The interior plaster work in progress

Below: The final touches. Our new architect John Taylor, had a great flare for the beautiful

The final stages outside

Connecting the drain with mains in Topsham Road. All the passing traffic knew something big was happening at St. Leonard's

Almost ready for use. Notice the entrance doors. These were the first ones, which shattered, and had to be completely re-designed
VI(D)

Above: Part of the superbly designed kitchen, with the fast washer in the fore-ground (right) and the gas stove (found on a tip and completely reconditioned, top left)
Right: A view from St. Leonard's Avenue
Bottom: Handing over the completed Centre by the Managing Director of Dudley Coles. Left, John Taylor (the Architect) and right Keith Bygraves (The Works Foreman)

At the heart of it all—Margaret Unsworth and Jean Burberry work in in the Parish Office (Church Vestry)

Left: Gordon Rice, Chairman of the Building Group, who made it all happen! Right: Mike Lane, Centre: Peter Elsworthy who led a team of active supporters with Sybil Vine

(5)   The beautiful tapestry includes the names of 637 people, who were regular church members at the time. This painstaking work was undertaken by a team, led by Anita Beasley, in whose home they met, and included Enid Govier, Chris Davis, Barbara Jackson, Margaret Dodds, Shanne Lane, Winifred Chapman, Margarite Jackson, Pam Williams and Ann Pyne.

(6)   Including regulars like Pam Williams, Enid Govier, Jean Burbury and many other willing helpers drawn in on peak occasions.

The Lay Assistants, also played a very significant role, helping with the 101 practical things as well as their other duties within the church, under Margaret's maternal eye! The first one, Ben Harris, started work just eight days after the fire and was immediately thrown in the deep end. He made an immediate impact on the Church family with his willingness and cheerfulness. We had been considering having Lay Assistants for some time, but we hardly anticipated the Lord's perfect timing as to when they would actually start! Those who followed in Ben's footsteps, over the next 5 years of upheaval were Tim Garrett, Emily Schnurr, Amanda King, John Gooddy and Orlando Saer, with his wife Libby.

(1)   The Imps (3-5) were led by Jo Rice, Hazel Davis and Shiela Maye,   Explorers (5-7) by John and Joy Hill and Sarah Branton,   Adventurers (7-10) by Gordon Rice, Phil Butt and Sarah Pritchard, Boy Jucos (10-12) = Junior Covenanters, by Graham Ireland and Willie Hunter, and Covenanters (13-15) by David Banks.

All these groups met in the Roberts Road Hall, with over 100 children altogether. Some, from the local area, were quite unruly, having been sent by their parents, who were desperate for a quiet hour on Sunday mornings!   The church referred to them as "the lost army" for they were sadly never seen again.

Apart from those who met in the Hall, the Girl Jucos, (10-12) led by Hilary and Graham Dixon met in a room in the Church Tower, and the Contact Group (15-18) were led by Joyce Hocking and Gill Lubbock and met on Friday and Sunday evenings either in homes or at the Hocking's farm at Pocombe Bridge.

Sometimes as many as 30 girl Jucos would squash into their den in the Upper Tower Room, using the high window sills as extra seating. There are still remnants of Juco activities on the walls today!

(2)   Reconditioned when George Bevington was Rector from 1960-1983

(3)   Many young couples were also starting families. From April 1986 - April 1987, for instance, there were twelve babies born, as reported in the Rector's Review at the Church ACM.

(4)   Built in 1966 for £6,000, with money from the sale of a site in Roberts Road

(5)   Tom Davis had a brilliant idea to try to find slightly more extra space.   He made several large, free-standing wooden panels hinged together, to channel the congregation away from crawling children, as they came in and out of church.   We were that desperate for every square foot of space! See the picture on page IV(A) where the panels are in place behind Sheila Goldswain, who was helping to supervise the children that day.

(6)   The Working Group consisted of Gordon Rice (Chairman), Tom Davis, (Architect and PCC Vice Chairman), Graham Dixon (Surveyor), John Hill (Architect and PCC Secretary), Joy Ireland (Crèche Organiser), Sheila Stirling (Secretary), John Willcocks (PCC Member) and the Rector.   Several others were co-opted later including Andrew Crossley (Surveyor).

Throughout the refurbishment and construction work, John Hill acted as the Church liaison link with the firms concerned and very generously gave of his   time and experience by attending all the many site meetings. We were particularly indebted to him.

(7)   Joy Ireland, married to Graham, and daughter of Sheila Goldswain had a remarkable and dedicated home ministry fostering a great many needy children, short or long-term over very many years.   There were 63 altogether, most of whom went on to adoption.

(8)   Assisted by Mary Brice, Jean Newman, Bridget Shiel and Shiela Maye.

(9)   To bring some of the children nearer to their parents, we had permission to use the modern premises of our local Central Middle Church of England School.

The Adventurers met in the Assembly Hall, and we were able to use the front playground for some of our parking. This helped, among other things, to alleviate the shortage of parking in Roberts Road. For some other church meetings we were able to go to 3, Claremont Grove at the kind invitation of Donald and Elaine Orchard.

(10) In 1987

(11) Including a tall sycamore tree near the allotments and several mature holm oaks skirting the old graveyard. Some readers will also remember a lovely magnolia tree alongside the approach to the foyer. When the allotments were considered as a possible alternative site for buildings (there were no trees there!), the problem was access for construction work. This seemed to be solved when number 26, St. Leonard's Avenue suddenly came on the

market, which could not only provide access alongside, but could also provide a home for our new Lay Assistant right next door to the church. We were immediately in a position to purchase it (at £64,000) with money from the sale of Trinity Church Hall, which came into our possession when St. Leonard's was originally linked with Holy Trinity in South Street, and was opposite the Salvation Army Citadel in Friar's Gate (£90,000). See map on page VIII (A)

(12)   The Planning Department stated that "their preference was for no more building at all on the church site", but they would allow us to, if we could improve the "hideous existing Foyer". One suggestion of theirs was to have a sloping roof instead of a flat roof, but this was only a cosmetic solution to help solve their dislike of the building anyway. For us, it would have done nothing to solve the root problem, which was shortage of space. They also came up with another alternative which Alan Anderson rejected as a "supermarket style" of development. Whatever the end result was to be, it was made clear to us that there would be no second chance, no "second bite of the cherry", with any other additions subsequently. Absolutely nothing further could be allowed. Incidentally, one consequence of having a flat roof was that it encouraged potential burglars (of whom there have been very many over the years) to gain access to the church through upper windows. After several such break-ins into the tower, Tom Davies devised a pattern of iron work inside (which could be clearly seen from outside) to frustrate them. It succeeded.

(13) This was God's perfect solution in <u>our</u> particular situation. Clearly in other church circumstances, equally desperate for radical change, he may well have different and more appropriate answers to equally fervent prayers. In my own past experience, for example, he chose to use the active presence of death watch beetle, which, when discovered, had to be dealt with extremely urgently. This coincided with our need for change and expansion, and occurred in a very old church mentioned in the Doomsday Book. In another Victorian church, God's answer, under similar pressure, was the sudden availability of land adjoining the church, on a tight site, owned by the City Council. They had a big re-development scheme and urgently needed a slice of the nearby Vicarage garden. They offered the land next to the church as a quid pro quo! Their requirements and the timing fitted exactly with our own urgent needs. So God always knows best!

(1)   Tracey Nichols, who had been a member of our Girl Juco Group. She alerted Alan Stevens, our newly arrived Curate, as well as the Emergency Services. Alan was, in fact, the first person to arrive on the scene. We discovered later that an intruder had set fire to the piano, by dropping a match in the back (the piano had been donated by Geoff Hobden, a Curate at St. Leonard's from 1982-1985). Only the cast iron frame and an iron umbrella stand survived.

In the next 10 days, incidentally, there were 2 further fires started, presumably, by the same arsonist. One was setting alight a large pile of rubbish cleared from the burnt-out foyer, and the other was between the First and Central Middle Schools.

(2)   Sam and Barbara Roberts, who were an example to us all of practical Christian Service, had cleaned the Foyer and the church that afternoon before the fire. They left the connecting doors (The 'Chesterfield doors' in the memory of Clive Chesterfield who had been a stalwart Youth Leader in our Contact Group) open, to assist the free circulation of air, little realising the crucial effect this would have that night. Imagine their dismay, the next morning to hear about the smoke damage to the church interior, which might have been prevented if the doors had been closed. In the event, the Lord used even this to hasten the complete refurbishment of the Church! Sam and Barbara were also our energetic Missionary Reps, for the South American Missionary Society. Sam later became a Church Warden.

(3) At one stage, at the height of the fire, the fire crew wanted urgent access to the Church interior. They were just about to hack the solid West Doors, when a voice shouted "Hold it - I've got a key!" It was Gordon Rice, who saved the day - and our precious doors.

(4) Made by Jean Hurford, Chris Davies and Jenny Rumsey.

(5) We had immediate visits from the Express and Echo for pictures and interviews, and from the Assessors acting for the Ecclesiastical Insurance Company. They took the unprecedented step - so we gathered later from John Richards the Archdeacon of Exeter - of giving us a cheque for £10,000 as an immediate float. How amazed, and deeply grateful we were for their practical concern for our needs.

(6) For Fred Wellington of West Grove Road. The Service was transferred hurriedly to Whitestone a village 3 miles away, where the burial was going to follow anyway.

(7) On the recommendation of Bill Sprague (of Sprague and Ousley), we contacted the Supreme Cleaning Service of Marsh Barton. They were willing to call in all their extra staff for such emergencies, and worked flat out for 2 days to complete a fantastic and highly professional job! The flower arranging team, led by Joy Hill, Mary Banks and Shiela Maye, managed magnificently that day (and subsequently) and their efforts made such a difference!

(8) From 1 Corinthians 3:9-17

(1)   The Royal West of England School for the Deaf was founded in 1828 and there have always been the closest links with St. Leonard's. Former Curates acted as   Hon. Chaplains and up to the 1960's children who were Boarders used to attend the first half of Sunday Services, occupying the chairs down the South side aisle.

Later the school held their regular Friday morning assemblies in church.   Non-boarders arrived by bus from all over the Southern Region and the Midlands on Monday mornings, returning after lunch on Friday afternoons. Latterly the school catered for those who were blind/or disabled as well as the deaf.

In the early days (i.e. pre the mid 60's) all teaching was through lip-reading and no signing was ever allowed. This was to enable children to integrate more easily with ordinary society outside school. This was my first experience of the school as its Hon.Chaplain there, during my time as a Curate at St. Leonard's, 1957-62, when Edric Royds was Rector. Subsequently, signing was introduced as the norm.

(2)   All the Building Group gave their time and expertise so willingly - and shared their vision for the wider project. They were a great team! John Hill was one who managed somehow to fit in his total involvement with everything right from the outset with his full time job as a working architect, with his own practice. He gave detailed help in relation to the insurance claim, he was the church liaison

person with both contactors, and attended countless site meetings. Gordon Rice regarded him as his right hand man. He was always reliable and rarely flustered. How he also managed to be the Secretary of the PCC, a violinist in the church orchestra, and chauffeur his harp-playing daughter around to her various concerts we shall never know! Needless to say we were immensely grateful to him and all the members of the Building Group for their huge contribution, and we thank God for them.

(3)   Later to become Bishop of Ebbsfleet, the first 'flying bishop' appointed to minister in those parishes unable to accept women's ministry. He covered the whole of the Southern half of England!

(4)   Some of the finely carved choir stalls we re-located at the back of the church.   Some of the old furniture had to go, including the high free-standing pulpit (see photograph on page 1(A). For our records, Tom Davis produced an excellent folder of photographs, which was circulated to those who might be interested in having it - including some American Bishops for churches in their diocese. Meanwhile Brian Power kindly stored it in his barn at Westcott Farm

We also had a small white free-standing statue of St. Leonard (the patron saint of prisoners), which had been kept in the tower. He was completely blackened through the fire, and it seemed appropriate to keep him that way, as a reminder of what we had been through. Unfortunately (or otherwise!) the cleaning firm who worked on the blackened stonework, used him to test out the effectiveness of their strong cleaning fluid. He was restored to his original whiteness, before we could intervene.

(5) In the end the Insurance Claim which covered the church and the Foyer was settled for £100,000 which paid for the church interior costs and the chairs. At first the Insurers wanted us to rebuild the Foyer, but a report by Jeffrey Try stated that the high-level concrete ring beam was so severely damaged that the whole Foyer should be demolished.

(6) John Searle was our other Lay Reader, later to be ordained in 1995.

(7) See what the Macedonian churches did in 2 Corinthians 8 : 1-9!

(8) The group 'Flaming Tongues' consisted of David Griffiths (guitar and vocals), Tim Roberts (drums), Mark Robertson (guitar), and the late Robin Howell-Phippiard (bass guitar). David himself composed all the songs.

(9) Graham Tomlin left St. Leonard's to become Chaplain of Jesus College, Oxford and Lecturer at Wycliffe Hall Theological College, where he was Vice-Principal and is now Principal of a Theological College at Holy Trinity-Brompton in London. Graham was succeeded as Curate by Alan Stephens, who did so much to establish the active group for 19-23's. This was a rapidly growing 'bridge group' not only for those too old for Contact but also for

those not going off to College.

(10)   From 1990 Gill Behenna became Chaplain of the Devon Deaf Community and had special links with the school and personal links with St. Leonard's. She has now moved on to the Bristol Diocese to do similar work.

(11)   For Kate Skinner, my daughter, and David Evans on March 31st and Penny Gray and Paul Dawson on April 28th . At the first of these I did the double walk myself on the way in, in my primary role as father of the bride.

(1)   We were very dependent on the Music Group at this time (augmented for special occasions). It included Millie Bailey, Rachel Cockram, David Gillett, John Higgs, Judith Feltham, Jo Coles, Jacqueline Herbert, Alison Head, Roger Moss and many others. We were richly endowed with musical talent!

(2)   In Luke 15:8-10. The elderly lady, aged 80, was Marjorie McLennan, the younger of the two sisters who lived on the corner of Wonford Road. She died aged 93 in January 2004 at the Woodhayes Nursing Home.

(3)   This wonderful provision came about through the good offices of Patrick Beasley, who was a Senior Consultant at the Royal Devon and Exeter Hospital and one of our members, and hosted (with Anita) one of the Student groups at that time, the Lynx Group.

(4)   There were a few dissenting voices over the colour scheme . One member expressed his strong views, "Don't like the carpet!" he said, but the vast majority were heartily in favour. One or two critics quickly became the strongest converts. Many of the old pine wood-blocks from the floor were taken into store by Hansford's and later re-used in the Church Hall, Roberts Road.

(5)   Matthew 18 : 19-20

(1) To have the professional expertise and enthusiasm of Jonathan Porter-Goff, one of our members, was a great bonus! As one of the Directors of Stage Electrics, his knowledge and flair made such a difference both for our overall lighting system and our P.A. Tirelessly he gave of his time and energies.

(2) A well-known Christian Professional Theatre Company based at St. Michael le Belfrey, York, who visited St. Leonard's a number of times with their productions.

(3) Andrew and Robyn Connett, Lorraine Butt and Tom Maye were part of the regular team which was augmented by one of the Home Groups each month.

(4) For the first time there was no immediate access to toilets! We therefore hired two Portaloos and put them well out of sight at the back of the tower, though getting to them especially in the dark at night proved quite a hazard. However we discovered later that they were not 'out of sight'. The steady procession of people was watched, with some amusement by those attending official functions just over Larkbeare Road in the Judges Lodgings. It was probably a good job none of us realised this at the time!

(5) The firm was run by Michael Farley, based at Kersbrook, Budleigh Salterton. The cost came to £12,698. 23, covered by insurance. The extra - mainly lowering the pitch and adding the Cremona Stop - amounting to £1,970.47, was paid for by the church.

(6)   The only surviving item remaining for future use was the cast-iron umbrella stand, now just inside the Entrance Hall and still in full use!

(7)   Easter 1991.

(1)   This was, in fact, a fair description, and typical of early 1960's architecture.

(2)   This first mention of the "Church Centre" was significant. Prior to this it was referred to as "the extension", "the Foyer" or just "accommodation".

(3)   We were able to visit St. Matthias, Torquay for a Church Away-Day. They had just completed their new Church Centre and gave us many good ideas. One of the key things we discovered was that it was already proving too small for their growing needs and they were already planning for an extension! They urged us to 'think big' to allow for expansion. It was to prove valuable advice. They were most gracious and stimulating hosts!

(4)   To test opinions within the Church Family a lengthy-Questionnaire was circulated. The results were carefully considered, showing a broad agreement with what was happening, but with (naturally) some dissenting voices.

(5)   See her 'Treasurer's Perspective' in the Special Appendix.

(6)   The four Charitable Trusts were the Maurice Laing Foundation, the Dame Violet Wills Evangelistic Trust in Bristol, (at the suggestion of Alec Motyer, one of their Trustees and a regular visiting preacher at St. Leonard's), the Dean Box Fund, (administered by the Cathedral Dean and Chapter), and the local Exeter branch of Natwest Bank from their charitable fund, through the good offices

The splendid Entrance Hall

The Welcome Desk (left), the magnificent banner with names of all the Churchmembers at the time woven into it, and the connecting doors to the Church

The Lounge downstairs could be sub divided with sound proof partitions for various children's groups. The hatch and door to the kitchen can be seen in the background, and one of the mission notice boards on the right

I(E)

The team, under the leadership of Anita Beasley (left foreground) who painstakingly produced the magnificent banner

The Bishop of Exeter (Hewlett Thompson) making his way, with considerable difficulty, through the sea of children...

...who then (with Diana King) led him on a tour of the whole building (from top to bottom)

...ending up in the main Lounge for the conclusion of the inspiring Service of Dedication

One of the many receptions for local residents (road by road)
hosted by Church members living in these roads. Right: Peter and
Ginny Hocking who hosted the crèche in their home until the
Centre was completed

Some of the kitchen team! (left to right) Barbara Marley,
Rosemary Sammons, Pam Williams and Bea Kealey

One of the upper rooms used by the Covies led by Betty
Cunliffe and Paul Hayward

IV(E)

Top: Graham and Hilary Dixon (long serving Girl Juco Leaders) and Bridget Shiel (One of the crèche organisers)

Right: Dorothy Armstrong (One of the Explorers Leaders) and Maggie Barker (Leader of the Counselling Team, and with her husband Charles, The Marriage Preparation Team)

Below: John and Sheila Stirling, flanked by Sylvia and Louis Muddleton, who work with Transworld Radio

V(E)

Children queueing for one of the brilliant Holiday Clubs

Children registering in the entrance hall. The large team of 40 wore the yellow sweat shirts

Purposeful activity for some of the young ones

VI(E)

Above: The upstairs rooms, with their sloping, attic-style ceiling were where the children felt most at home. That flat roof greatly enhanced the building too!

Right: Close-up of the new welcome desk in the entrance hall, specially designed and created professionally by Robin Furlong one of the Furlong family (Derek, Heather and brother Simon) who were all very active at St. Leonard's, as well as in the Exeter Crusaders

Above: Rev Howard Cunnnington (Curate who followed Alan Stevens) Bottom: Welcoming all ages (0-90?) in the Entrance Hall

VII(E)

Above: A reminder of the very first church on the St Leonard's site. Demolished in 1830
Right: With the spire pointing church members and parishioners in the right direction
Below: The present day church with spire

of former manager John Hutchinson, member of St. Leonard's and father of Rosie Button, (a St. Leonard's Missionary), and Andy Hutchinson, (Holiday Club Leader).

(7)   The Earl of Northcliffe (back from India) laid the Foundation Stone under the East window on August 18th 1876.

(8)   Barings was sold to the Dutch Bank, ING, for £1.

(1)   John Taylor, who is on the far left of the picture on page VII (D) had a smooth handover from Alan Anderson, and admired what had been done already in the refurbishment of the church interior. When he first saw it he just stood there taking it all in, before saying "Wow!" He was also most gracious in inviting a large group of us into his own home one Sunday afternoon to hear our suggestions on colour and design.   As we looked round his home, with its beautiful and tasteful décor, we hardly needed to say anything. We all knew we had the right man for the job!

His main assistant, Ken Brasher, chaired the monthly site meetings and was concerned with most of the nitty gritty of the project.

Tom Davis, who retired as a county architect for East Devon in 1984, now came into his own, yet again, in designing the kitchen in close consultation with Heather Furlong and June Skinner. He was immensely versatile, having a hand in much of the church refurbishment, especially the church heating system for which he had become quite an expert over the years. He also produced meticulous drawings of the church pulpit with photographs to match, and dealt with the serious dry rot which subsequently developed (Sept. '94) in the platform at the front of the church, which was made good by Hansfords free of charge. Now in the Church Centre design, he turned his expertise towards getting exactly the right facilities for the present and future use of the big main kitchen and the upstairs kitchenette. He spent hours in consultation to   *1* ensure everything was considered for the biggest and smallest occasion. One issue, for example, was the amount of crockery needed and the speed at which it could be washed up and re-used immediately. He not only discovered a fast dishwasher that could clean 25 cups in 90 seconds, but also a generous, anonymous donor who would foot the bill of £1,771.20. This was yet another example of self-effacing generosity which was developing throughout the church family, and exemplified by Tom himself. For instance, he was quite horrified, even a few days before he died in November 2004, at the thought that his name might crop up in this manuscript. "Cross me out" he said to me. His faith, already strong, grew still further over raising the huge sum of money (in those days, if less so today) to pay for the Centre. At one stage, he told me, he thought £250,000 was the absolute upper limit that St. Leonard's was capable of raising, but his faith grew by leaps and bounds and was amply rewarded. The church owes an immense debt of gratitude to Tom, who had the professional skills, the available time (after retirement), the unbounded enthusiasm and the deep personal trust in the Lord he served so well.

There is a story behind the large 6-burner cooker too. It was rescued from a skip and was completely transformed by 50 hours of vigorous cleaning by a determined team!   •

(2)   It was ready for viewing on Sunday, January 24,1993

(3)   A lower ground-floor youth room, below the

'allotment' corner was seriously considered at one stage, although it would involve considerable extra excavation and possible disturbance of graves. The cost, however, would have amounted to a fifth of the total cost for this one item, and it was considered to be too prohibitive to include. Sadly, therefore, it had to be ruled out.

(4)   This enthusiastic team included Margaret Curry, Liz Hosegood (former midwife) and Sybil Vine who came up with all sorts of ideas. The wide variety of events included a concert by the internationally renowned trumpeter, Crispian Steele-Perkins, who had grown up in the parish, and whose family had very close links with the church, another by Cantilena Choir, one of whose members was Juliet Meadowcroft. These all proved most happy and worthwhile occasions and introduced many visitors to all that was happening at St. Leonard's.

(1)   This semi-attic design has given real character to these first floor rooms, where children's groups feel particularly at home. They are also the rooms specifically booked by outside groups, and are served by an upstairs kitchenette and toilets.

(2)   Minster Stone, who produced 12 block types and sizes. The builders had to work to a 'random spread' chart to produce the right blending effect.

(3)   We were also able, through a revised cost plan, to save a further £59,200 from the estimate figure.

(4)   By a subsidiary of Pilkington Glass in Germany.

(5)   The question of whether VAT was payable or not caused us considerable problems. Gordon Rice wrote to me on May 9th 1991, "I went to the VAT Office this morning. I saw a third person. I explained the letter I left and said I would call back shortly. I got a third (and of course) a different answer. I am supplying yet more details. I think I am still sane."

Eventually, after much patient discussion, it was established that if the new building was attached to the church, as a listed building still in use, there would be no VAT payable. If it was not attached to the church and used by a charity providing facilities for a local community, no VAT was liable. However if part of the old Foyer was repaired, replaced or renewed and then used, VAT was payable on that part. We demolished the old Foyer completely and paid no VAT!

(6)   Tenders were opened on May 24th 1993 at the offices of Bailey Widrel, the Quantity Surveyors in Southernhay. The tender prices varied between £467,167 and £510,641.

(7)   James 1:3-6

(1)   We came across several early burials in unmarked and unrecorded graves.   These were all reverently re-interred nearby.

(2)   Second-hand slates were carefully selected to blend in.

(3)   Some time after the new Church Centre was handed over to us, someone was carrying a TV set through the glass entrance doors - made of armour plated glass - when one of them suddenly shattered. Everyone was astounded, including John Taylor, and the manufacturers could not understand what had happened. Each of the 4 doors was hung on 2 hinges fitted to the glass, but none of the doors had a frame. Negotiations for its replacement had not been finished when a further mishap occurred. The children from the Royal School for the Deaf were coming in for their weekly Friday morning Service. One 7- year old boy pushed on one of the remaining 3 doors and it too shattered, sprinkling him with small pieces of glass. He had to go back to the school immediately for a complete change of clothes and a bath, and we were greatly relieved that he was not injured in any way.

The manufacturers were mystified and we were horrified. John Taylor then designed 4 new doors, with frames this time. However before they were delivered the manufacturers went into liquidation. There were problems over responsibility because they were the nominated sub-contractors within the overall contract with Dudley Coles. We expected to make an arrangement with the Liquidators of the company because the doors had been made specifically for us and it was most unlikely that they would suit anyone else's requirements. We waited, we enquired, we probed. The weeks became months and well over a year passed. Gordon finally established where the doors were, and when in Bristol called to see them. After further delay, a new company came down to fit them. Expectations were high! At long last something was happening. Even the delivery men seemed pleased, as they carefully unloaded the new doors. Imagine everyone's dismay when they found that even these didn't fit - and had to be reloaded and taken back to Bristol.

Eventually, the saga ended when new doors arrived and these are the ones in place today. Altogether it had taken much longer to get these replacements than it did to build the Centre!

(1)   Great credit is due to the construction firm Dudley Coles who did a first-class job. Their experienced foreman Keith Bygraves, who was a pleasure to work with (together with Ray Paramore their Contracts Manager), showed great sensitivity in working on a church site, where church activities were in full swing all around him. We are grateful to God for providing us with such a firm. See picture on page VII (D)

(2)   Roy Henderson had also served as Chairman of the Patronage Board of the Church Pastoral-Aid Society for 25 years. The Board are responsible for presentations of new Vicars in 500 or so evangelical parishes throughout the country, including St. Leonard's as our Patrons.

(3)   The catering team were led by Heather Furlong, with numerous members including Lorraine Butt, June Skinner, Barbara Marley, Hazel Davis, Rosemary Sammons, Sybil Vine, Sue Cockram, Freda Greenwood, Faye Rickard, Rachel Snellgrove, Norman and Esther Goodfellow, Ginny Hocking, Pam Williams, Anita Beasley, Shiela Maye.
Other Church Centre teams were the Cleaning Team - Jean Burbury, Sylvia Stroud, Vic Houghton; the Counselling Team - Maggie Barker and Sheila Grove; the Practical Team - Mike Lane, Christopher Clapham (who made all the notice boards and shelves) and Spencer Unsworth. Charles Barker was the Centre Administrator.   Mark Robertson provided all the new shrubs around the Centre, and Phil Butt and Richard Eales continued to keep the church grounds tidy.

(1)   Mary Brice was a much loved and greatly valued 'granny figure' for several generations of children.

(2)   The new Creche team was led by Margaret Curry and there were sometimes up to 30 tiny children to look after week by week. Among her many regular helpers were Lorraine Butt, Julie Slade, Liz Searle, Jean Newman, Bridget Shiel, Margaret Hartnup, Carol-Ann Shabytah, Ginny Hocking and Barbara Jackson.

(3)   Making hundreds of cups of tea for workmen on site and constant visitors was just one aspect of 'serving the Lord' in a practical way!

(4)   ICE – The Initiative in Christian Education, a team set up by Colin Piper taking C.U. meetings and assemblies in all the local secondary schools in the city. Other missionary societies included the Church Missionary Society (CMS), the South American Missionary Society (SAMS), TEAR Fund. Wycliffe Bible Translators, Trans-World Radio, Crosslinks and the Leprosy Mission.

(5)   There is also a small counselling/prayer room on the upper floor which was well used. We were greatly indebted to Maggie Barker, the leader of our Counselling Team, as are the countless people who have been greatly helped and encouraged by her sensitivity and discernment. Both she and Charles gave themselves totally and wholeheartedly in this work both in the Centre and in their home. For many years too, they led the Marriage Preparation Courses for all those married at St. Leonard's.

During these three sessions they made such close friendships with the couples (some living in the parish, of
course, with no regular church background) that they were
personally invited as guests to their weddings.   Both
Charles and Maggie have been widely used by the Lord at
St. Leonard's in a whole variety of roles, and we thank
God for sustaining them throughout.

Other outreach groups making full use of the premises
were, for example, the Craft Group, led by Jean Hurford
and Freda Greenwood, and the Young Mums Bible Study
Group.

(6)   Norman Shiel, apart from all his other roles, (for
example) as editor of the St. Leonard's Neighbourhood
News and City Councillor (this year, 2006, as Mayor), has
been a most diligent and efficient Hall Bookings Secretary.

(7)   One alarming incident took place three weeks after
we took over the Centre. On Sunday morning it was discovered that part of the ground floor was flooded. What
had happened was that vandals had taken the allotments
hose pipe, pushed it through the overflow pipe from the
ground floor Men's Toilets and turned the tap on. Emergency mopping up was carried out, and with the help of
some industrial driers the Hall was reasonably dried out.
However the concrete floor took a long time drying out
and many times we had to take up the carpet tiles to allow
the concrete to breathe, and then relay the tiles in time for
the next use of the Hall.

(8)   John 15 : 5 and Philippians 4 : 13

(1)   1 Timothy 2 : 3-6—see John 3:16

(2)   Tom Davis (CMS), Sam Roberts (SAMS), Jean Hurford (Crosslinks), Andrew Grove (TWR), David Smith
(OMF), Iain Coldham (Leprosy Mission), Alison Black-
well –nee Mansell (Tear Fund), June Skinner (Bible
Society) and Fiona Caldwell (Wycliffe Bible Translators)

(3)   What might have happened had this initial test been
failed? Perhaps the outcome would have been very different? Only God knows.

(4)   Ephesians 3 : 20-21

(5)   Acts 20:35 See also 2 Corinthians 8 : 1-9

(6)   John 13 : 34-35

(7)   Tim Chesters in 'The Message of Prayer' (IVP)

(8)   Romans 5 : 5

(9)   The Christian writer David Bosch

(10)   God's work in his people summed up in 2 verses :

"We have this treasure (the knowledge of God in the face
of Jesus Christ) in jars of clay to show that this all-
surpassing power is from God and not from us"
2 Corinthians 4:7

"You are…..a people belonging to God that you may declare the praises of him who called you out of darkness into his wonderful light" 1. Peter 2:9

The foundation stone for the Church Centre reads

> *For the glory of God*
>
> *and the extension*
>
> *of his Kingdom*
>
> *1993 - 94*

NOTES

NOTES

NOTES